The Highly Intuitive Child

"Outlines 10 important skills that parents can teach intuitive children ranging from learning how to tell the difference between random fears and intuition, to how to turn down the volume on 'intuitive antennae.' Offers sincere support and practical information to parents searching to aid and more deeply understand their highly intuitive child."

— *Publishers Weekly*

"One of the most important gifts we can give our children is to help them trust themselves. When we trust ourselves, we possess an inner compass on life that no one can take away. I can't think of a better gift to give a child. May this book help in keeping the inner compass of intuition and empathy alive and thriving in our children."

— *From the book*

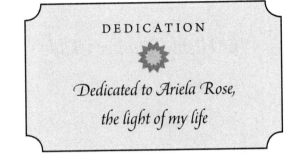

DEDICATION

Dedicated to Ariela Rose,
the light of my life

the highly intuitive child

a guide to understanding and parenting unusually sensitive and empathic children

Catherine Crawford, MFT, ATR

Hunter House PUBLISHERS

Hunter House Inc., Publishers
PO Box 2914
Alameda CA 94501-0914

Library of Congress Cataloging-in-Publication Data
Crawford, Catherine.
The highly intuitive child : a guide to understanding and parenting unusually sensitive and empathic children / Catherine Crawford. — 1st ed.
p. cm.
Includes bibliographical references and index.
ISBN-13: 978-0-89793-509-8 (pbk.)
ISBN-10: 0-89793-509-8 (pbk.)
1. Intuition.   2. Sensitivity (Personality trait)   3. Empathy in children.
4. Parenting.   I. Title.
BF315.5.C73 2008
155.45'5—dc22   2008031400

Project Credits

Cover Design: Brian Dittmar   Senior Marketing Associate:
Graphic Design   Reina Santana
Book Production: John McKercher   Publicity Intern: Sean Harvey
Copy Editor: Mary Miller   Rights Coordinator: Candace Groskreutz
Proofreader: John David Marion   Customer Service Manager:
Indexer: Nancy D. Peterson   Christina Sverdrup
Editor: Alexandra Mummery   Order Fulfillment: Washul Lakdhon
Editorial Intern: Kimberley Merriss   Administrator: Theresa Nelson
Editorial Intern: Ruoji Tang   Computer Support: Peter Eichelberger
Production Assistant: Amy Hagelin   Publisher: Kiran S. Rana

Printed and Bound by Bang Printing, Brainerd, Minnesota

Manufactured in the United States of America

9 8 7 6 5 4 3 2 1   First Edition   09 10 11 12 13

contents

chapter 4

when an intuitive child needs professional help

chapter 5

the care and keeping of intuitive, empathic bodies

chapter 6

boundaries

chapter 7

parenting the intuitive child 99

chapter 8

teaching the ten skills

chapter 9

**art, play, and spirit for
the intuitive child**

foreword

"We, the grown-ups, have failed you deplorably." These words were addressed to children throughout the world by the Secretary General of the United Nations, Kofi Annan, in 2002, and they highlight our failure to provide the "future of humanity" with basic needs for health and well-being. Although his focus was on protecting children from violence, poverty, and disease, the Secretary General's words could also be applied to providing for the emotional needs of children, particularly those with special sensitivities who do not adapt easily in today's stressful and unstable world.

Some experts have gone so far as to call today's children the "shell-shocked generation." Due to a broad range of stresses—divorce and family breakdown, crime and violence, drug abuse, overstimulating media, a failing school system, terrorism—an increasing number of children are suffering from emotional disorders and behavior problems.

Fortunately, there is a new awareness and interest in the special sensitivities of children and what is required for them to thrive emotionally, cognitively, and spiritually. For example, based on child development studies and brain research, we now know that some children are born with what I have termed "biological sensitivity." Known in research studies as "highly sensitive children" and "high reactors," such children are deeply affected by their emotional and physical environment. Psychologists have identified these sensitivities in children as young as four months of age, and they can predict which children will develop emotional problems, such as anxiety, by the time they begin school. On the positive side it has also been shown that when their parents respond skillfully, sensitive children can function at high levels of effectiveness and without the emotional difficulties that might otherwise develop.

"Intuition" is an unexplored aspect of children's sensitivity, and I am pleased to see that Catherine Crawford has accepted the task of researching and writing about this interesting subject. The result is a book that helps us to understand highly intuitive children and respond appropriately to nurture their unique gifts, help them achieve their potential, and even learn from them.

Catherine Crawford's book convincingly opens our minds to the reality of children's intuitive abilities. She reviews the science and provides the information we can use to recognize and support highly intuitive children, while helping us avoid the pitfalls involved in overlooking the special needs of such children. Crawford provides down-to-earth suggestions, real-world tips, and user-friendly guidelines.

I had the pleasure of meeting Catherine Crawford during her research and writing of this book. It was obvious to me that she is an experienced psychotherapist/art therapist who is attuned to the inner world of children. She is a credible and trustworthy guide on the journey to understanding highly intuitive children.

I hope this book reaches a wide audience of parents who will learn how to appreciate their intuitive children and how they as parents can nourish their children's special gifts. In addition, the information contained in this book will benefit virtually everyone who works with children, including educators, psychologists, social workers, psychotherapists, and health-care providers. Most of all, the children for whom this book was written will benefit from what the adults in their lives will learn about them.

— Paul Foxman, PhD

www.drfoxman.com

Dr. Foxman is author of *The Worried Child* and *Dancing with Fear*. He is the Founder and Director of the Center for Anxiety Disorders in Burlington, Vermont.

acknowledgments

This book was graced with incredible help from inception to finish. As a new author, the assistance of so many capable friends and guides proved indispensable. The process of writing a book is a solitary adventure but I was never alone. In fact, the conversations with friends, colleagues, experts, and interviewees kept the journey of writing this book dynamically alive. I cannot imagine writing this book without the tremendous support I have received for this project. I am grateful to all of you and thank you not only for supporting me, but also for supporting the children and families that this book seeks to serve.

Thanks to Judith Orloff, MD, for kicking off this project by suggesting that I write this book. Judith's suggestion is proof that we never know how personal destiny can unfold in a day!

Paul Foxman, PhD, heard the value of this book and suggested its home with Hunter House. Paul, if books come with godparents—you're it. I acknowledge the work and support of the generous and committed staff of Hunter House. Thank you Kiran Rana for believing in this project and helping to define its balanced message. Alex Mummery, Mary Miller, and Kimberley Merriss all helped trim, reframe, and clarify this book with their exceptional editorial expertise.

This book received early editorial assistance from four very special women: Annie Folger, Barbara Porro, Hansine Goran, and Marianne Palmer. Annie Folger and Barbara Porro, chosen sisters, heard the call of this book, held the vision, and never faltered in supporting me in this work through every step—every page. Hansine Goran not only consulted on numerous concepts and editing, but also her witnessing of my intuitive nature and potential is exactly what I hope every intuitive, empathic child on the planet can have the great fortune to receive. Marianne Palmer, dear friend and rarest blend of intuitive, feeler, and scientist, helped me bridge the worlds of science and intuition with tremendous commitment, insight, time, and kindness.

Thank you to the generosity of professional consultations with Tobin Hart, PhD; Steve Copeland; Bill Pfeiffer of Sacred Earth Network; Elizabeth Murphy, EdD; Lynn Horowitz; Betty Peck, EdD; Gail Fritz; Francine Brevetti; Beverly Martin; Dumari Dancoes; Rick Williams; and Robert Palmer, MD. Your contributions were essential in helping me expand and clarify my ideas. To those who generously gave interviews for this book—Matthew B. James, Mercedes B. Longfellow, Angangaaq, and Holly Guzman, OMD—my heartfelt thanks for blessing this book with an expanded perspective of life.

People often wonder how a working mom can write a book, and I can attest to the fact that we don't do it all by ourselves. We need help and I had plenty. I thank my beautiful, loving community of friends and family who support my life's journey. I couldn't have done this without you. I am grateful to all of you; in particular, I wish to thank and acknowledge the following people who gave uniquely to this project: the Crawford and Winkler clans, especially my loving parents, Lois Crawford and Renee and Ralph Winkler; Jody McCalmont; George Bruder; Diane and David Marcus; Jordan Gruber; Gail Slocum; Hilla Richards; Mike Goran; Maaike and Matthias Linnenkamp; Lisa Sgarlato; Kelly DeGrange; Nancy Field; and Laura Romanelli.

The greatest cocreator of this work is my husband, Brian Winkler. Brian, you helped shape this work—you and Ariela are the wind under my wings, and I couldn't have done it without all of your love and support. You've given me the gifts of time, supporting my life's work and holding the vision of this book. This book is ours because you are part of every page. Where I stumbled while bringing these ideas to clarity, you steadily and brilliantly helped me bring sentences, pages, and chapters into clear focus. Thank you for giving so fully of yourself.

I thank all the intuitive and empathic children and their families who have so generously shared their stories with me. Thank you also to all those whom I've worked with over two decades, those whose luminous examples of change and living their potentials inspire me to continue this work. I acknowledge the spirit of transformation alive on our planet today. May we, as adults, provide the best possible home for the children of today and the children to come.

Important Note

The material in this book is intended to provide a review of resources and information related to the parenting and support of intuitive children. Every effort has been made to provide accurate and dependable information. However, professionals in the field may have differing opinions and change is always taking place. Any of the treatments described herein should be undertaken only under the guidance of a licensed health-care practitioner. The author, editors, and publishers cannot be held responsible for any error, omission, professional disagreement, outdated material, or adverse outcomes that derive from the use of any of the treatments or information resources in this book, either in a program of self-care or under the care of a licensed practitioner.

introduction

The intuitive mind is a sacred gift and the rational mind
is a faithful servant. We have created a society that
honors the servant and has forgotten the gift.

ALBERT EINSTEIN

Welcome to *The Highly Intuitive Child*, a book that is designed to help parents and other caregivers understand children who are especially intuitive and empathic. Since you were drawn to this book for some reason, my guess is that you may already realize, or suspect, that you have a highly intuitive child in your life. Perhaps you are parenting a child who has demonstrated an uncanny capacity for intuition and you have some questions about your child for which you are having trouble finding answers. You might even be a bit perplexed, nervous, or excited about your child's intuitive abilities. I hope this book will answer some of your questions about highly intuitive children and provide the help, support, and guidance that you are looking for.

The Highly Intuitive Child is about children who are not only highly intuitive but highly empathic as well. Intuition involves the ability to pick up on subtle information that is not perceived directly through any of the five senses, but rather is detected through an invisible sixth sense. Empathy is the ability to tune in to how another person is feeling by registering those feelings through the body.

People who have both high intuition and empathy often sense unseen, emotional vibrations of other people through their own physical

1

and emotional systems. To illustrate, if you take a tuning fork, strike it, and then place another tuning fork of similar size next to it without having them touch, the unstruck tuning fork will begin to vibrate with the other one. *Intuitive empaths* not only sense the feelings of others acutely but also feel them so strongly that they tend to internalize them. Thus, it is important to help them learn, among other things, how to regulate their intuitive/empathic *"aperture"* so they aren't feeling burdened by everyone else's aches, pains, and moods. In this book, you'll learn why this happens and specific ways to help your child regulate these abilities better so they can enjoy more of the gifts and less of the challenges associated with these heightened abilities.

I believe that intuition and empathy are wonderful gifts to possess. Intuition can be a source of inner guidance, creativity, imagination, personal direction and meaning, a decision-making tool, and even a personal security system. Empathy helps us step into someone else's shoes and deeply feel what the other person is feeling. This capability gives rise to qualities such as kindness, compassion, and understanding, all of which can be immensely helpful in creating and sustaining successful relationships. Together, the qualities of intuition and empathy can be powerful allies on the journey of life.

Why seek out a book supporting children who have an extra degree of these abilities? Perhaps it is because children born with such a turbocharged sense of heightened empathic intuition can encounter some specific challenges relative to their heightened abilities. Despite all of the positive aspects, it is not always easy for the child or the parent to know how to deal with the many challenges that also come with this trait. For instance, what do you do when your child can tell that you're having a conflict with your spouse, even when not a word has been spoken about it to your child? What do you tell your child when they have intuitions of danger that turn out to be accurate? How can you help intuitive children when they feel a friend's pain so deeply they can't shake it off, feel responsible to fix and heal situations because they detect another's pain so acutely, absorb so much of a classroom's stress during the day that they have trouble falling asleep at night, get confused by conflicts and think that another person's feelings are actually their own, and even feel the pain of the world?

Much of this book is dedicated to helping your child learn how to deal with the unique challenges that are often part of the fabric of an intuitive child's life. You will learn why these challenges occur, the stress signals to look out for, and what to do to help comfort your child. Although not all intuitive children will experience stress related to their abilities, many do, and this book is intended to support and prepare you for those possibilities.

My Experience

I bring to this work my experience of being an intuitive child, and of working with highly intuitive children and adults as a psychotherapist. I am also a mother. As someone who is intuitive, empathic, and sensitive, I have cultivated the skills that I speak of in this book over decades of personal experience in both my personal and professional life. My experience as a marriage and family therapist and registered art therapist with twenty years of counseling experience has given me the opportunity to work with hundreds of clients of all ages and witness their intuitive insights firsthand. The book that you are about to read is the result of all of this experience, and I am enormously grateful to all of the people who have helped to shape this book and these insights by allowing me into their lives. The stories presented throughout this book are based on real-life experiences. In the case of my client's stories and personal experiences, specific identifying information has been changed to protect their identities.

My Inspiration for Writing this Book

The purpose of this book is to help prevent some of the difficulties that can typically happen when the needs of a highly intuitive, empathic child are not met. When I work with highly intuitive adults, I often find that as children they had to suppress and shut off their intuitive capabilities because of the negative reactions to their perceptions from family members and other important people in their lives. This frequently results in a disconnection to oneself, mistrust in one's inner guidance, shame, anxiety, or depression. Fortunately, this gift can come back to life, but experience has shown me that this can often demand a long healing process for the adult who learned in childhood to suppress his or her natural abilities.

We can prevent this kind of suffering by acknowledging these abilities in children, being willing to speak of them, and skillfully supporting their unique needs. To truly support highly intuitive children, we must understand intuition and not discount, judge, fear, or suppress it.

My inspiration for writing this book lies in my hopes for these and all children. Our children are our future scientists, politicians, doctors, leaders, educators, and healers. In an age when we need to find solutions to the problems that the world faces, and when the clock is ticking on issues such as global warming, poverty, health care, and more, how can we afford to discount the significant role intuition can play in life? Children deserve to have the full range of their gifts available to them when they launch into adult life. I believe that we owe the coming generation, whether highly intuitive or not, our full support for the gifts that they will bring to the world.

Pushing Past Barriers

We can't fully support intuitive children without being open to their experiences. For a variety of reasons, the topic of highly intuitive children has been largely missing from mainstream parenting and psychology books. Intuition is often the target of cynicism, doubt, and fear. Even modern psychology's founding father Sigmund Freud wrote that he feared talking about his own intuitive experiences because he did not want to be dismissed as a credible scientist. Still, he was fascinated with what he called *thought transference*, also known as telepathy. He struggled with his desire to pursue this further with colleagues who shared a similar interest and, ironically, ended up imposing silence on their research findings.[1] These kinds of fears result in difficulties exploring and talking about the issues that affect highly intuitive children in a meaningful way. *The Highly Intuitive Child* is intended to take some of the mystery out of a mysterious and often marginalized subject area so these children can receive the support and understanding they need.

Indigo Children

In their 1999 book *The Indigo Children*, Lee Carroll and Jan Tober identified a growing number of children possessing unusual characteristics and behaviors. Some of these traits include highly perceptive, intuitive, and original thinking, in addition to a sense of personal authority. Since the release of their book, many other authors have contributed to the indigo child concept, even branching off into new categories such as "crystal children" who, although similar to the indigo children, possess more empathic and sensitive qualities.

Highly intuitive children share some of these characteristics, especially those relating to intuitive, perceptive, and empathic qualities. Whether or not you believe in indigo or crystal children, it is apparent with the rising popularity of books dedicated to this subject area that there is a growing curiosity and openness to children's intuition.

The Highly Intuitive Child is unique in that it not only addresses identifying the traits of high intuition and empathy in certain children, but it also offers practical tools and advice to help them master the unique challenges that accompany these innate abilities.

My Approach

My approach is broad. You will find a chapter dedicated to what some indigenous tribes and communities around the world have to say about raising intuitive children. Road maps of how to raise intuitive children exist in our world but are largely absent in our modern-day lives. The stories of indigenous practices and wisdom serve as a reminder that we can change our dominant concepts about intuitive children by assimilating some of the wisdom that the world's wise elders lived by in raising children with these capabilities.

I advocate a real commonsense, down-to-earth approach to parenting highly intuitive kids. With this approach, you will find real skills from which you can pick and choose as needed with your child. These skills are designed to help your child feel more confident with her abilities and to reduce stress in problem areas. Many of the ten skills that you'll learn about in Chapter 8 are also expanded upon throughout the book. Wherever possible I try to interpret the invisible worlds of intuition and empathy into something accessible. You'll find ideas about using art and other creative tasks with intuitive kids. You'll find guided meditations with which you can lead your child as they learn to settle down a sensitive body system for sleep or learn how to meditate for stress management. And you'll find a whole chapter designed for supporting you, the most important person in your child's life, in taking great care of yourself so that you can continue to meet the needs of your child.

In the final chapter, I present a sneak preview of the journey ahead by comparing stories of intuitive adults who both received and were denied support of their abilities in childhood. In Chapter 11, you will see why it is never too late to reclaim the power of this trait by reading the transformational stories of adults who put these skills into practice and turned their suffering into strength.

Some Limits to this Work

I draw from decades of professional and personal experience for this work, but my research is strictly anecdotal, not based on quantified research. The research I share from the field of neurobiology, as in the implications of mirror neuron research on understanding empathy, is also relatively new, and many of the links to this subject matter remain to be proven. Early work on the connections, however, is promising, and I think new insights in this area might prove to be important components in understanding some possible biological factors for highly empathic children in particular.

This book is in no way a complete picture of the complexity and richness of intuitive children's lives. I see it as a launching point for those who are interested in learning how to recognize, appreciate, guide, and support highly intuitive children with both love and practical skills. I hope that it gives rise to further thinking and support for these children.

An Invitation

I invite you to take your time and allow your children to take their time in learning how to come into balance with their intuitive development. No parts of this process can be learned rapidly or exactly. We all are exquisitely unique, and I encourage you to use your own judgment and instinct in how you utilize this information. Take what works and leave the rest.

I have tried to keep the different strengths of parents in mind while writing this book. We are as diverse as our children. Whether you are a parent who shares your child's abilities and is looking for additional help, or whether you do not share these heightened abilities in common with your child, I hope this book speaks to you and offers useful explanations and ideas.

I believe that one of the most important gifts we can give our children is to help them trust themselves. When we trust ourselves, we possess an inner compass on life that no one can take away. I can't think of a better gift to give a child. May this book help in keeping the inner compass of intuition and empathy alive and thriving in our children.

who is the
highly intuitive child?

*It is always with excitement that I wake up in the morning
wondering what my intuition will toss up to me, like gifts
from the sea. I work with it and rely on it. It's my partner.*

JONAS SALK

The road to adulthood is not always a smooth one for the highly intuitive child. Accurately sensing other people's thoughts or feelings, or sensing impending danger, may be overwhelming for a young child. This is especially true in our post-9/11 world. My experience as a psychotherapist has taught me that as highly intuitive children grow up, they may become overwhelmed or marginalized, which may lead to negative psychological consequences that carry over into adulthood. This suffering can be prevented. Giving these children what they need when they need it helps to ensure the experience of heightened intuition is a gift rather than a burden. In order to accomplish this, we need to understand the world of intuitive children and extend to them our love, acceptance, and skillful guidance.

This book explores what it means to be a child born today with turbocharged intuitive and empathic capabilities. Although it may be tempting to think of highly intuitive children as being quite rare, this is not the case. I meet these children often, hear about their joys and struggles, and hear the questions from countless parents on how to best meet their unique needs. It is often difficult to recognize a highly intuitive child in a classroom or on the soccer field because they can be quite adept at keeping their insights to themselves and they usually come across as being a typical child. Often their abilities fly under the radar of most adults and other kids. The reasons for this privacy are many, but one of the biggest reasons for these children tending to keep their unique insights private is their keen observation that they are aware of things that most people are not.

Many parents wish their child came with an instruction manual—no matter what their traits and temperaments. This can certainly be true when it comes to trying to meet the needs of a highly intuitive child. The challenges of raising a highly intuitive child fall outside parenting norms. Not only is there very little written on parenting intuitive children, but intuition itself is often an unfamiliar or even frightening realm.

Defining Intuition and Empathy

Everyone is born with intuitive capabilities: knowing something at the gut level without, or before, confirmation. A mother's intuition helps her translate the meaning of her baby's cry and a businessperson may know a business deal is going nowhere by an empty, sinking feeling in his stomach—long before he has the data to substantiate the feeling.

Intuition attracts a wide and often controversial range of responses in people. Most people have had intuitive experiences. A surprisingly large number of important discoveries are the result of intuition and not just deductive reasoning. All people also share the ability to demonstrate empathy, or the ability to project ourselves into another's feelings, situation, or thoughts. Empathy emerges as a vicarious experience as we put ourselves into another's world.

We all experience intuition and empathy in varying degrees. This book is designed to help children who experience more of these qualities and with greater frequency. These children can especially benefit from having support that is specifically tailored to their unique experiences in life. Being highly intuitive doesn't mean that every child will experience the same characteristics, abilities, or even stressors; these vary greatly. Even children who are frequently impacted by intuitive and empathic input will vary greatly in the degree to which it affects their lives. Some children will float in and out of the characteristics that I present in this book, while others seem to live in these realities on a much more full-time basis.

A Gift Set to the "On" Position

What distinguishes the highly intuitive child from others is a matter of degree. Unlike an innate gift that is intentionally cultivated (for example, the ability to compose music or create art), an intuitive child's gift is always in the "on" position whether or not it has been cultivated. It is also turned on whether the child wants it or not. It is a trait that influences everything one experiences in day-to-day life. The influences of a turbo-charged intuition can affect a child's biology, stress levels, relationships, views on spirituality, and sense of personal meaning.

I believe that highly intuitive, empathic children are born with this ability and that it is a function of nature, not simply nurture. Because they start life with these abilities, in this book I will be framing my discussion of these abilities with words such as *trait* and *gift*, which seem to be a good linguistic match for these inborn abilities.[1]

All children are gifted in their own ways and valuable beyond measure. The purpose of this book isn't to set apart this group of children as "special" or "better" than children who experience less intuition and empathy in life. It is simply designed to get to know the needs of these children who experience *more* intuition, *more* frequently.

Stronger Intuition or Empathy Can Make a Difference

Most of this book is dedicated to the times when intuition is paired with empathy, but there are also portions of the book that focus on one more than the other. You might find that your own child's experiences ebb and flow between these two abilities as well, which is very natural. For example, your child might be very intuitive with moderate empathic ability or highly empathic with moderate intuitive ability. The combination can vary widely. Children who lead with intuition may have more occasions of knowing something to be true from the sixth sense and experience challenges particularly related to how they deal with energetic boundaries, which you will learn about in the boundary chapter (Chapter 6). Children who lead with empathy experience heightened perceptions of how other people feel in their own bodies. Especially empathic kids are born with a heightened ability to naturally attune to other people's needs, and their challenges lean toward paying attention to their interpersonal boundaries. For example, they need to learn to pay attention to what they themselves want and need instead of always tuning in to and acting on other people's needs. Children who experience heightened ability in both of these areas need help in regulating the potential stressors of both so they can enjoy the full benefits that intuition and empathy can provide.

I personally lean more toward being highly empathic, with intuition coming in as a strong second. As I've attended to managing empathic stressors (such as being particularly aware of what other people are feeling and needing) and putting the ten skills taught in this book into action, it has had the effect of sharpening my intuition. Sometimes my intuition takes the lead; sometimes it is empathy. You may find the same to be true for your child, and this book is designed to take these variances into account.

Intuitive Thinkers vs. Intuitive Feelers

People with high levels of intuition typically fall into two subsets: *intuitive empaths* and *intuitive thinkers*. Intuitive thinkers, like Thomas Edison and Albert Einstein, experience and express their intuitive insights through cognitive channels. Einstein took an intuitive quantum leap in his thinking and ascertained the theory of relativity without first making a step-by-step rational analysis. It wasn't until after he had leaped to the intuitive conclusion of this theory that he then employed rational cause-and-effect thinking to help explain it to the rest of the world. Einstein is a great example of intuition and rational thinking working in concert with each other and of the power of intuitive thinking.

Intuitive empaths, on the other hand, experience intuition through their body and emotions. There are overlaps between these two kinds of intuition, but the vast majority of this book concerns intuitive empaths; when I speak of intuitive children, I am speaking in shorthand of the intuitive empathic (IE) child.

The world is finally warming up to how intuition can play a role in situations such as scientific breakthroughs, but it appears a bit slower to warm up to the role of intuition as it commingles with empathy in a person's life. I think this is largely because our culture still favors thinking over feeling. When intuition and empathy are combined, the experience is typically a visceral feeling, or a gut instinct, that gives us information about people, safety, and bodily truths that say, "it's a YES" or "it's a big NO."

We are all intuitive, just as we are all thinkers. But people differ in the degree to which they possess these abilities as dominant functions within their personality. The Swiss psychiatrist Carl Jung brought this variance to our attention in the last century in his work involving personality typing. Jung's ideas were popularized through their application in the Myers-Briggs Type Indicator test that is now used widely in therapy, business, and education.

The popular Myers-Briggs typology test for adults was designed to determine whether or not a person possesses more sensate, feeling, thinking, or intuitive ways of approaching decision making and style of being in the world. It assesses for strong tendencies in one of the four areas but also highlights the need to develop the weaker tendencies in order to live a balanced life. The test has been so helpful in the workplace and other settings that it is still widely used today. Managers have learned in the business world that they benefit from knowing and positively integrating an employee's primary style of learning and interacting with other people—information that is revealed in the test. Likewise, parents can benefit from knowing the primary style of their child and adapting around their strengths.

Jung added a great deal of depth to our understanding of the difference between spontaneous knowing that emerges from unseen sources, or intuitive knowing, and what has come to be known as sensate knowing, or the experience of knowing something through your tangible five senses. According to the Meyer's-Briggs test, the sensing/sensate function involves what can be experienced through the five senses, whereas the intuitive function has the ability to see the big picture, or the *gestalt,* in any given situation. Although the intuitive type in Jung's model has many parallels with the type of intuition I am describing in this book, it is not an exact match. In addition to his view on the intuitive function, I also weave in the concepts of the ability to sense invisible "vibrational waves" of energy-containing information.

Intuition in Action

There are many true stories about young children who shock, amaze, and sometimes even frighten their parents with their intuitive impressions. Take Amy's 2-year-old daughter, Deanna, for example.

✳ Deanna — age 2
Toddler's Intuition Warns Mom

One day Amy was taking Deanna to a toddler playgroup for the first time. As they drove down the long, winding driveway, Deanna exclaimed, "Watch out for the chickens!" Looking around the clear driveway, Amy asked, "What chickens, Deanna? There aren't any chickens, honey." Deanna continued to insist on chickens. While Amy enjoyed her 2-year-old's wonderful imagination, around the next curve she was shocked to find not one but four chickens pecking around on their neighbor's driveway.

Neither Deanna nor Amy had any prior knowledge that this family kept chickens; what happened that day was an example of intuition at work. For many young intuitive children who haven't yet been taught to deny its presence, intuition can be a normal, matter-of-fact way of receiving information about life. Some would call it clairvoyant knowing, psychic, a sixth sense, or just plain intuition. When we experience an impression or sense of "knowing" outside the linear, rational thinking process, we call it intuition.

When Amy spotted the chickens that her daughter had warned her about, she knew she had a child with an extra helping of intuition.

A child's communication of intuitive information may bring up varied responses in the parent. The chicken story could be chalked up to coincidence and tucked away as a random funny story. Others might be scared of having their child speak about intuitive hunches and communicate a fearful message to their child. Another response may be intrigue combined with the desire to know more about how a 2-year-old child could predict things with such accuracy and perhaps how to work with this trait if it comes up again.

Predicting chickens in the road is a comical and benign way to be introduced to a child's keen intuitive abilities. But what happens when a child starts to pick up on bad feelings between Mom and Dad or the neighbor—and begins to talk about it? When a child innocently reports intuitive observations that adults would prefer kept hidden, it can leave a parent feeling stunned. Some well-intentioned parents try to turn off the valve of intuitive knowing in a child, afraid that such perceptions bring trouble in life. If you have experienced a child's intuition, or this strikes a chord in your own history, perhaps you can relate to the variety of reactions provoked by an intuitive child's insights.

Highly intuitive children experience life quite differently from their sensate-focused peers. Sensate-focused children are very comfortable with the physical dimension and can dive into life and zoom from activity to activity without much need for reflective processing. The sensate-focused child excels in moving through life as experienced through the five senses. By contrast, intuitives are more focused on their inner world, taking in a huge volume of information through the unseen sixth sense, as well as the data from the other five senses like their peers. The extra data can be stressful to juggle, and they often need much more downtime to integrate the additional perceptions.

Here are two examples that illustrate the differences.

✳ Dan — age 7

A Day in the Life of a Sensate-Focused Child

Dan is a high-energy, sensate-focused boy who is rarely bothered by events that have nothing to do with him. He bounds out of bed in the morning, hops into any clothes he can find, gobbles down his breakfast, and is off for another day's adventure. He's excited because after school is baseball and pizza with his best friend, Joey. School is extra noisy because there are two kids fighting today, but it doesn't bother him. Nor does the fact that the teacher is in a bad mood and "loses it" with a couple of the kids. During recess his friend Pete breaks his arm. Dan is concerned for a few minutes, but quickly forgets about it after Pete goes to the school nurse. The day blazes along, and finally when it is time to go to sleep, he is out like a light soon after his head hits the pillow, feeling little need for reflecting on the events of the day with his mom and dad.

Now let's consider an intuitive, empathic, sensitive child at the same school in the same class.

✳ Andrew — age 7

A Day in the Life of a Highly Intuitive Empath

Andrew is having a challenging morning. He's having difficulty getting out of bed because he had a bad dream about someone at school getting hurt and it leaves him with a bad feeling that he cannot shake. Worse yet, it reminds him of some waking daydreams he had about people he loves getting hurt—which actually came true.

He tells his mother about his feelings and his mother tries to comfort him by telling him it was just a dream. But he still feels a knot in his stomach. He gets dressed. The tag inside his shirt and the seams in his socks are driving him crazy. His mom gets him a shirt without a label in the back and some seamless socks. At school, Andrew is unnerved when he experiences two kids fighting. It is noisy. He can feel the anger between them, as it begins to take the form of a pain in his head. When his grumpy teacher "loses it" with two noisy kids, his entire body tenses up. He goes out to the playground for recess, and it is difficult to shake the feeling from the classroom. When he witnesses a classmate injuring his arm, Andrew's arm throbs with pain for several minutes. Later that evening, Andrew is having difficulty falling asleep. He is bombarded by swirling images and feelings from his day. His mother tries to get him to fall asleep with a back rub and kind, comforting words, but even those remedies aren't working, and it is now far past his bedtime. Andrew tells her about the events of the day, but also about his fears of death and worries about people hurting and killing each other in some other country.

Intuitive children can be a sponge to life, experiencing feelings in their environment (and even somewhere else on the planet) so deeply that it can influence moods and even body chemistry as it did for Andrew. Because they experience the feelings of others so strongly through their emotions and body, they tend to have an unusually large dose of empathy for kids their own age. They are often highlighted in school as the caring kid who others can go to for some help and understanding. However, the reverse can be true if the child's stress levels max out, causing the child to act out the pain and frustration that she is picking up on. Children with a sensate focus seem to have more of a Teflon coating to life's pain, and they are often less likely to feel or be concerned about the pain of others. This is not to say that this temperament style is not sensitive to the needs of others, but it does appear they are often less physically sensitive and spend less time with concerns of the "inner life."

This does not mean that intuitive children are more valuable or more evolved; they simply are tuned in to a different frequency. Indeed, there is a lot that intuitives can learn from sensate children, and vice versa.

How Do You Know If You Have an Intuitive Child?

So far we have focused on defining some of the unique characteristics of an intuitive child. As you read this book, you may be wondering if your child is one. Although I am reluctant to create a new label or box to fit children into, there is value in having a common language we can use to discuss the gifts and challenges inherent to heightened intuition.

twenty questions to ask yourself if you think you have an intuitive child

The questions listed below reflect some of the similar kinds of experiences various parents notice in their highly intuitive children. Although they are not designed as a diagnostic tool and are not exhaustive by any means, they can give you a flavor of some of the distinctive qualities.

1. Does your child have a way of finishing your sentences and reading your mind?

2. Is he bothered by conflict and does he prefer harmonious relationships?

3. Does your child have an ability to "see" things before they happen?

4. Does she pick up on the feelings in a room or place and possibly act them out?

5. Is he prone to headaches and stomachaches related to other people's stress?

6. Do loud noises and crowded places bother her, causing her to change moods?

7. Can he feel tension between his parents even if they are being tight-lipped about it?

8. Does she feel tension during traumatic world events, maybe even drawing pictures of them or spontaneously talking about them with no knowledge of the events?

9. Does he have an active inner life, including talking with fairies, a guardian angel, or imaginary friends?

10. Does she have a frequent need to be in nature for quiet reflection and the recharging of her inner batteries?

11. Does he report feeling different from his peers?

12. Does she have a fascination with the meanings of life and death?

13. Did he exhibit the traits of high intuition and/or empathy at an early age with no instruction?

14. Is it hard to keep a secret or surprise from her? Does she guess her birthday present?

15. Does he have an instinctive knowing of what younger children or animals need and translate those needs for you?

16. Do calm feelings, less activity if overstimulated, a peaceful environment, and kind honest words soothe her?

17. Does he have a high level of sensitivity?

18. Is she able to come to solutions at times with surprising, inexplicable speed?

19. Does he know about how people feel regardless of physical distance?

20. Does she have a tendency to make connections about other people and the world that outpace developmental norms?

The Strengths of Being an Intuitive Child

One of the most important things we can do for our intuitive children is to help them see the gift of their intuition. Their insights can guide them to act in ways that are deeply fulfilling, simplifying key decision-making times throughout life. When they learn how to sense the truth about something by listening to their intuitive guidance, they begin to anchor a sense of "true north" in their life. Intuition can provide your child with keen insights about other people, helping them to be more socially successful. And in a world where we must teach children the awareness of dangerous people and situations, they can use their sixth sense to steer clear of danger and stay safe. Intuitive children have a lovely understanding of what other people need and have a knack for helping and being present to others. Many can translate the unspoken needs of babies, toddlers, and animals. And in the words of one intuitive child, they "know what others need and can connect with the universe."

To illustrate, let me tell you about Christina.

✳ Christina — age 5

Using Intuition to Interpret an Animal's Needs

Christina is an exquisite, bright, and verbally gifted 5-year-old. She is also very intuitive. I learned this information from speaking with her and listening to her tell me about her cat. She told me that she always knew when Barley was hungry or hurt before anyone else in her family knew. When she was asked how she knew this information, she responded, "I have a little tickle inside of me that tells me." Intuition can work that way in children, and it is wonderful when they trust the data that comes from their bodies. She is fortunate to have parents who appreciate and take her intuition seriously, and who give her the opportunity to explore and cultivate it (and I'm sure her cat appreciates it as well!). Christina also possesses another commonly held characteristic of many highly intuitive kids: She asks big and unusual questions of the adults in her life. Even at the age of 5, she asks questions like, "Can you tell me about where your spirit was before you were here?" or, "What does it feel like to fall back into your spirit at death?" And on a humorous note, she asked her young 3-year-old cousin not to lose the tricycle she passed along to her because "she'll be needing it in her next lifetime"!

How Your Parental Response to Your Children Impacts Their Lives

A parent's attitudes and acceptance of their child is one of the most important factors in the life of every child. You are your child's first teacher and the person who gives comfort, safety, and the reassurance that not only are they *okay*, they are wonderful! When gifted, intuitive children experience stress for whatever reason, it is a deep comfort for them to come home to people who accept them unconditionally and are present to hear about their experiences.

I've learned in my work with adult intuitive clients that the client's perceived level of support and acceptance that they received from one or both parents, especially concerning their extra sensing capabilities, had deep and lasting effects. If, as a child, the person grew up feeling loved, seen, heard, and accepted, it contributes to the individual's resilience in handling tricky situations out in the world and his ability to design a life that is inner-directed. If the child's gifts were marginalized and criticized, then the adult may face the task of recovering his intuition, rebuilding self-trust, and nurturing deep self-esteem that allows them to be truly comfortable in life with this set of gifts.

As I mentioned earlier in the chapter, the gifts of intuition and empathy are there whether the intuitive person wants them or not. Try as the person may to stamp them out, these gifts just won't go away. With a gift that informs so much about how a child moves through life, I think it makes clear sense to acknowledge the gift for what it is and find a way to be in harmony with it. As parents, the first step of being able to support these unique children with learning the extra adaptive skills they will need begins with a positive attitude toward the child and their unique way of seeing and feeling in life.

One of the hallmarks of building self-esteem in children is letting them know they are truly seen and valued. This empowers them and makes them feel strong in their bodies and grounded in life. Self-esteem grows when we let children know that we love them, no matter what, for who they are. When we follow a child's lead with questions that show interest or empathize with her feelings, we are bringing our presence without judgment to the relationship. In the case of intuitive children, we can respond to their experiences with a kind, open heart, even though we can't see or prove the data they are drawing from. When children don't feel understood, they remain hungry for this need to be fulfilled, often long into adulthood.

One of the problems with having a highly intuitive child, if you don't share this gift, is that it can be hard to deeply understand and see the child's experience. The majority of parents lead from a place of sensate awareness. If you see life more through the sensate lens, and not through the intuitive lens, you might have times when it is hard to understand what your child is talking about when he shares his intuitive experiences. When they are very young, their intuitions might sound more like the world of imaginary play and stories, but as these children enter elementary-school age and their peers tell them their intuitive experiences are weird and not real, how is the sensate-focused parent supposed to respond to these perceptions in the child? I find that this critical developmental stage emerges when the intuitive child begins asking himself the question, "Do I continue to speak about my experiences, or do I conform to what my friends think is true?" If parents are unwilling to offer a safe landing place for their child's impressions and intuitive insights at home, the child can face even more stress.

When intuitive children get the impression that the adults they depend on think they are overly sensitive, weird, occupy too much of their time, or should act more like other kids, they may be tempted to start to shut down. Unfortunately, as they try to suppress their gifts, they start to shut down other wonderful parts of the self. The cost is great for children who detect, register, and believe that their trait is too much for the people around them. In the child's mind, this is a message that her whole self is too much. It is at this unfortunate point that an authentic sense of self is injured and the child may begin to develop a pseudo-self to fit in with the world. Ultimately, I don't think this trait can be quashed or taken away. My work with adult intuitives teaches me over and over that the gifts of intuitive empathy cannot be lost. When repressed in childhood, these intuitive gifts wait under the surface until they can be seen, acknowledged, and given permission to be used again.

One of the purposes of this book is to make sure the gifts of intuitive empathy do not go underground and that these children receive all of the unique support they need in life. Preparing children for their inevitable launch from home requires the mastery of so many life competencies. Although all children share the need for many common life skills as they move toward adulthood, I believe highly intuitive children can benefit from mastering ten extra skills, or competencies.

Overview of the Ten Important Life Skills for Intuitive Children

What follows is an overview of my ideas on the skills intuitive children need to learn, or at least begin to learn, before they leave home as young adults. The development and application of these skills can be found in the skills chapter (Chapter 8). These skills can take well into adulthood to master, so I encourage patience both with your child and yourself as you teach these ideas and work with them.

1. **Learning to tell the difference between random fears and intuition:** It is important to learn how to distinguish between an intuition and a random feeling or fear.

2. **Regulating the intuitive antenna:** Intuitive children are capable of gathering impressions, feelings, and even telepathy from sources far and wide. In order to feel less bombarded or overwhelmed, it is important to learn how to regulate the intuitive antenna.

3. **Turning down the volume on the extrasensing system:** These children need to know how to turn their attention from other people, events, and environments to go deep within themselves. They need to learn how to turn down the volume on this input. This way they know they can have a break from high stimulus in the world.

4. **Cultivating an intuitive vocabulary:** It is important for you and your child to have a vocabulary for speaking about intuitive insights and abilities, and to know how to find people who can be supportive of these experiences.

5. **Paying attention to what you need and want:** Intuitive kids are very adept at perceiving and responding to other people's needs, and it is essential to counterbalance this tendency by paying close attention to personal needs, speaking up for these needs, and cultivating a lifelong practice of taking great care of themselves.

6. **Practicing daily energy hygiene skills:** Intuitive children need to know how to clear out the feelings that they might have taken on during the day so they don't feel depleted by them or start to act them out.

7. **Staying grounded:** It is important for the child to feel safe and connected to the earth, also known as being grounded. The skills for grounding are supported in the child through personal acceptance, a sense of belonging, and connection to others.

8. **Distinguishing your energy from that of others:** It is important for intuitive children to know how to distinguish their energy and feelings from those of others so that they are not regularly taking on other people's feelings and stressors. An example of putting this into practice is to ask the question, "Is this feeling mine, or does it belong to someone else?"

9. **Handling faulty intuitive conclusions/checking facts:** Intuitive leaps can be faulty sometimes and driven by imagined meanings where none exist. Intuitive children often need help remembering to engage their rational, fact-finding skills to verify their intuitive conclusions. This skill helps in reducing anxiety and interpersonal stress associated with faulty intuitive leaps.

10. **Incorporating intuitive empathy into everyday life:** Intuitive children need to integrate this trait into a healthy sense of self as they mature. The deep roots of physical and emotional security nourish the blossoming of intuition in a balanced and beautiful way.

Throughout the book, you'll learn more about why I developed this list of life skills based on the challenges these children can face, why they need our help, and how to help them develop these competencies. By the end of the book, I hope you will have the confidence to weave all of these skills (and more!) into life with your child. With ample support, your magnificent, intuitive child will thrive.

common challenges
faced by intuitive children

*The power of intuitive understanding will protect you
from harm until the end of your days.*

Lao Tzu, 600 BC

The gift of intuition is so present in these children's lives that sometimes they have trouble regulating the heavy flow of incoming data.
Feeling other people's emotions or physical sensations (also known as
somatic empathy), digesting telepathic flashes of danger, and detecting
what is left unspoken by parents, teachers, and friends can be challenging for these children. This information can overwhelm and outpace
their developmental abilities to process it, leaving them feeling scared,
anxious, confused, depressed, and even in psychosomatic pain. The intensity of the data inflow can stress the nervous system and result in the
child feeling uncomfortable physically.

Parents of highly intuitive children often wish that intuitive data
could be more clear-cut. Unfortunately, that is not always the case. It is
quite natural to mix up intuition with random fears and unconscious
projections about other people. Sorting through this input can be tricky
for both parents and children. As with the learning of all life skills, it is
important to take your time and expect to experience a learning curve.
Sometimes parents of intuitive children are caught entirely by surprise,
as illustrated in the following story.

✳ **Anna — age 7**

A Mom Learns to Trust Her Daughter's Intuition

Anna and her mom, Jenny, were busy with their late afternoon activities. Anna was busily moving from one creative project to the next while her mom was in the kitchen making dinner. Both were in a calm frame of mind and enjoying a seemingly carefree day.

All of a sudden, Anna came to her mother and said with great urgency and clarity, "Mom, there is a very bad man out on our street and I want you to lock all of the doors." Jenny listened to her daughter's concerns, and although she took no action, she was not entirely dismissive. Jenny, a savvy education specialist in her late thirties, knew enough to let her daughter express her feelings and try to help her become more comfortable. Internally, she wrote off the warning because she thought it was a manifestation of the worries that often plagued her daughter. "Poor kid," she thought to herself. "I need to get her more help for her anxiety. I better read that book on child anxiety on my nightstand."

Anna was irritated by her mother's efforts to calm her feelings. She saw right through her mother and knew she was giving her that "feelings talk" again. She tried it again louder. "MOM! Lock the doors! I am telling you that there is a bad man out there. I feel creepy and tingly and I know there is some sort of danger!" By now she was following her mom around the house and didn't want her mother to leave her sight. She also insisted that her mom not go outside.

Jenny started to think this was odd. She grew especially concerned that Anna was having "creepy and tingly" physical sensations that she hadn't been having a few minutes prior to this whole drama. But she stayed firmly planted in her conviction to work harder on helping her child work through her irrational fears. When all of her usual methods to comfort her daughter failed to restore her peace of mind, she turned on the TV and hoped a cartoon would distract her long enough to get dinner onto the table.

Two hours later a neighbor called. "Jenny," she said in somewhat of a quiet panic so that her own family wouldn't overhear her on the phone and be frightened, "we have an emergency situation in our neighborhood. A fugitive just shot and killed two men and he is on foot in our neighborhood. There is a manhunt for him, and the police have shut down the streets. Lock your doors and don't go outside."

Jenny was in shock. While she quickly locked the doors and lowered the curtains, astute Anna wanted to know why Mom was suddenly taking her seriously. Jenny tried to look calm but once again Anna could see through it. She lit into her mom with questions: "Who was that on the phone?" "What did they say?" "I know you are hiding something from me!"

In between giving Anna short, unsatisfying statements to buy more time, Jenny was slipping behind closed doors to call and warn other neighbors. By now, Anna came straight out to her mom and said with poise, clarity, and a no-nonsense tone of voice, "I think you should tell me the truth."

Jenny had a huge decision to make and she was feeling out of sorts herself. Both she and her daughter were in the middle of a neighborhood where a manhunt was being conducted. It was dangerous. She realized that she had not honored her daughter's deep intuitive warning of danger and didn't want to go further in being dismissive of her daughter's intuition. In fact, while Jenny had often noticed her daughter's striking intuitions, she had always held some skepticism about whether or not they could be real.

The confirmation of the fugitive manhunt gave Jenny irrefutable evidence that her daughter had the capacity for incredibly specific intuition. Jenny's mind was working in overdrive concerning her new realization about her daughter and the added punch of adrenaline in her own system. Jenny tried hard to think as clearly as possible. She saw this situation as a teachable moment to give her daughter honest feedback, so she took a deep breath and confessed, "Anna, you were right. There is a bad man out there and the police are taking care of the danger and will find him." Anna was quiet for a moment, looked deep into her mom's eyes, and said a calm voice, "Thank you."

Jenny and her daughter had a direct experience of how the power of intuition can help to keep us safe. In Gavin de Becker's book *The Gift of Fear*, he teaches that intuition is exactly what can keep us out of dangerous situations. De Becker is one of America's leading experts on predicting violent behavior and crime. As a three-time presidential appointee on evaluating threats on political officials, as well as being an adviser to media personalities, business leaders, and other important community leaders, he is the "go-to" person on predicting violence. He doesn't mince words when it comes to the power of our intuition when he states, "It is a process more extraordinary and ultimately more logical in the natural order than the most fantastic computer calculation. It is our most complex cognitive process and at the same time the simplest."[1] With a seamless blend of rational and intuitive insight, his message is a compelling one whether you lean more toward the rational or toward the intuitive. He has shocking evidence from decades of experience that indicates people routinely deny their intuitive warning signals, thus putting themselves right into the hand of danger. He states, "Americans worship logic, even when it's wrong, and deny intuition, even when it's right."[2]

Jenny didn't act on her daughter's warning initially because she fell prey to a typical behavior of well-meaning, well-educated parents everywhere. She explained away her daughter's experience based on her own rational explanation of this behavioral anomaly. Jenny had good reasons to do so. Anna had an active imagination and was prone to worry. Jenny immediately started to explain away the anomaly based on what her own mind was most familiar with seeing. I imagine she also didn't want to have to deal with a possible "bad man out on the street," or what it would mean to her sense of reality to know that her own innocent 7-year-old could pick up on information of this nature.

Anna's request was simple and clear: Lock the doors. It wasn't outlandish. She wasn't asking her mom to do something that would negatively impact other people, look silly, or require significant amounts of time. She just needed to know that the house was safe. Jenny had very little to risk by just locking the doors, and potentially she had a lot to risk by denying her daughter's warning. Weighing the risks involved, it seems it would have made logical sense to heed her daughter's intuition.

While Jenny was trying to figure out the probability of the situation being a real intuition or a random worry in her daughter, she was losing precious time and potentially failing to keep her own daughter safe. She was also engaging in another behavior that De Becker warns most often puts us in danger: failing to listen to our own instincts and talking ourselves out of what we know to be true. In order to stay safe, he teaches that we need to always pay attention to the times when our intuition sounds off with true fear.[3] True fear looks, feels, and sounds very different from worry or anxiety. The latter are typically ruminations of the mind that pull our attention out to a future time. "Oh, I'm worried that I won't pass that test in two weeks." "What if my friends don't like me anymore when I wear that outfit?" By contrast, "Lock the door now, there is a bad man out there!" has a sense of the immediacy. The intuition is clear, but interpreting the message is more complex.

Jenny and Anna's story is a dramatic one, but the lessons it holds about intuitive, empathic kids are many. Next, we'll take a look at how to use this story to help you tease out the differences between intuitive hunches and random fears, how to handle situations like this one as a parent, and what it teaches us about the challenges faced by intuitive children.

Telling the Difference Between Intuitions and Random Fears

Sometimes it is challenging to differentiate between an intuition and a random fear that comes from the imagination. I want to give you ideas on ways to recognize the signals that you or your child is in the zone of an intuitive truth. We'll do this by studying Jenny's story for clues.

Here are the specific clues that indicated Anna was experiencing a specific intuition instead of a random fear:

- ★ **An abrupt change in mood with the incoming intuition:** Anna was in a great mood and happily engaged in her typical play patterns. When she "got" this intuition of the fugitive, her whole demeanor changed rapidly.

- ★ **The child feels danger in the body:** Anna described for her mom that she felt a creepy feeling in her body. Her body gave her signals of danger that she couldn't quite explain rationally, but she knew to be true.

- ★ **A sense of immediacy:** Anna was adamant that her mom lock the doors immediately. She didn't mince words; she was clear and consistent. She didn't continue to embellish the story with further details, as we would expect with a story that is generated by the imagination. Anna was prone to imaginary tales but this experience was more of a declarative warning. It was absolutely different from her imaginary yarns, or the more typical childhood fixations on fears like, "Turn on the light; there's a monster under my bed!"

Telling the Truth and Protecting Our Children

By deciding to tell her daughter the truth regarding the fugitive at large, Jenny was leaping into uncharted parenting territory. She had never read about what to do in a situation like this one, and it didn't seem right to compound her daughter's fear. Her husband was away on a business trip and out of cell phone range; ultimately, Jenny felt a clear sense that her daughter should know her warning had been correct. It would be an important lesson in communicating the difference between the sense of intuitive urgency in this case compared with ordinary fears. Jenny's lesson was to listen to her own inner voice, which told her Anna's intuition was right. Together they could discuss how this experience was different from just a passing worry by investigating the intuitive and physical signals that emerged for Anna.

As a parent and as a therapist, I believe in honesty with children. But we also don't want to burden children with information that is developmentally inappropriate. Intuitive kids are famous for stumbling into subject matter or asking questions that indicate they are more developmentally sophisticated than we would expect. In Anna's case, the candid answer that her mom gave could have caused anxiety and worry, and it is a striking example of a situation that we'd hope no 7-year-old would have to deal with. If you have a child who leans toward anxiety, you have the additional challenge of sifting through how to handle situations like this one in a way that doesn't elicit more anxiety.

Let's look at some other helpful ways Jenny could have responded to Anna's sudden intuition of danger. Jenny could have said, "I can see that you are very serious about this, Anna, and I want you to feel safe. Let's go and lock all the doors together." Taking this action would have given Anna the message that she was not only heard, but that Mom was willing to take specific actions to keep her safe. It would have been a message that her mom trusted her intuition. Even if the intuition was wrong, it would have been a simple enough action to take. Next, they could have spent some time together doing a calming activity to help get their minds off the fear. When the call came in verifying Anna's warning, Jenny could have been much more discreet. Of course, all of these alternative measures that could have been taken to help mitigate Anna's anxiety are more easily seen with the wisdom of hindsight. In that moment, Jenny did the best she could do for her daughter, given a multitude of competing needs.

Intuitive children often press for answers until they hear the truth, or until they receive an answer that feels congruous with what they are experiencing internally. For example, if your answer to them is a half-truth or even a lie, they might look at you and say, "Are you sure that's how it went?" or, "Oh, come on, you're not telling me the whole thing and I know it!" When the neighbor's call came in, Jenny first tried to put Anna off, but Anna detected her mom was hiding something. She wouldn't take no for an answer. In the end, Jenny decided to let Anna know that her intuition was correct so that she had real-time learning of the validity of her intuitive hunch. The benefit of intuitive confirmation outweighed the potential risk of creating worry for her daughter.

Challenges at School for the Intuitive Child

Intuitive children often have a knack for knowing how to behave and what others need from them. These kids can be a real dream for teachers in the classroom. They can be the model student who is even depended upon to help restore balance with peers who are acting out in the classroom. However, it might be harder than it looks for the intuitive child in the classroom.

The child may be quick to know what the other students or teacher needs for balance to be restored, but being constantly relied upon in this way can be a real stress factor for the child. The intuitive child can become fatigued from overgiving, overfeeling, doing more than is developmentally appropriate, and even ramping up into adult communication skills that are better left for adults. In short, they can work too hard. This is especially true in classrooms where teachers and school systems aren't operating on the principles that create healthy, open communication where a child's social and emotional needs are valued. Intuitive children tend to know these principles instinctively, and when adults and systems aren't holding up to what these children feel is possible for their friends and themselves, it can leave them feeling frustrated, angry, anxious, and sad, or even lead to them acting these frustrations out in the classroom.

One of the telltale signs that intuitive children are working too hard at school with their intuitive, empathic abilities is that they fall apart when they get home. This book will teach you the signs of stress to look for in your child and specific ideas on how to support your child. Occasionally, the match of teacher, and even school, for the child is one that needs to be reviewed and possibly changed for the child to feel safe, calm, and focused on learning.

Magical Thinking vs. Intuition

Of all of the challenges highly intuitive children face, magical thinking can be one of the trickiest to sort out. We all start out in life with magical thinking that is developmentally right on target. A child looks up at the moon, sees what appears to be a smile on its surface, and magically thinks the moon is smiling at her. The child's cognitive process gathers together a couple of pieces of information and jumps to the conclusion that the moon is in a special relationship with the child—and she alone is the center of the moon-and-I relationship. This classic magical-thinking snapshot is not only appropriate in a toddler and preschooler, but it can also be quite delightful to witness. It is important to address how true intuition can be written off as simply magical thinking. If we lump all of a child's intuitive impressions into the category of magical thinking, even when they are accurate beyond any doubt, we muddy the distinction between intuition and imagination. It is important to know the difference so that you can tailor your parenting support directly to the challenges of magical thinking or intuitive perception.

Magical thinking can be high-octane fuel for creative imagination. It can also be fuel for faulty cognitions. For example, a child might see a shadow in the bedroom at night and become convinced that it is a robber lying in wait to do harm as soon as the child falls asleep. Suddenly, the few pieces of data gathered via night vision may seem to coalesce into an *intuitive impression* that there is someone in the bedroom. Details blur into a faulty intuitive conclusion that is fueled by magical thinking.

All children (and adults) are capable of magical thinking, so what is the distinctive issue for highly intuitive children? As a natural cognitive style, these children naturally jump to intuitive conclusions much more than sensate children. Although this cognitive leaping is a tremendous asset in brainstorming, seeing the bigger picture, and quickly understanding systems or complex relationships, it can be a deficit if those quickly generated intuitions are faulty. Negative magical thinking throws a monkey wrench into clear thinking. Learning to tell the difference between magical thinking and a clear intuition is not always easy, but you can help as a parent if you know what to look for.

Magical thinking can feel a lot like jumping to an intuitive conclusion, but it is different. Intuition has a distinct "signature" of arrival; the body signals a sense of inner knowing even without necessarily seeing anything immediately—hair might stand on end on the back of the neck or a sudden image pops into the mind. Magical thinking, on the other hand, seems to piece together details that create a faulty picture of reality. The child sees the outline of clothing shadows and soon is convinced not only of the robber but a full-scale assault on the family. This is magical thinking run amok. Ultimately, the way to determine the difference between intuitive impressions and a magical thinking tangle is to check the facts. Most intuitive kids don't readily check for facts in order to know the difference. It can be a big blind spot. You can help your child out of magical thinking corners by gently having him work backward to check the facts and details of whatever it is he is convinced is occurring.

Understanding the Intuitive Antenna

Intuition often involves picking up on information that does not come in through one of the five senses. Anna's intuition of the fugitive is a perfect example because she had no tangible experience from her five senses to alert her to the danger. She wasn't even responding to a direct empathic response set off by being in close physical proximity to danger. Her intuition came in simply and clearly on the invisible sixth sense channel.

I realize that it can be challenging to try to understand a system that is literally invisible, so I'd like to explain this next concept by comparing it to a television antenna (perhaps a somewhat outdated analogy given that we now live in the cable/satellite era, but still very relevant regarding intuition). A hundred years ago, if someone told you that invisible waves would someday fly through the air, would be attracted by a metal lightning rod of sorts (antenna), and then the wave impulses would go through the antenna into a box and come out as pictures and sounds, you would have thought that person was nuts. You would have thought that person was even more nuts if he told you these waves would manifest in different channels with different pictures and sounds through the box depending on how you turned a knob, or "tuned" it.

Today almost no one in the world would question the existence of television waves, the resulting pictures and sounds, and the various channels in which these waves manifest, even though many people do not understand how they actually work (including me).

This television antenna example is similar to how intuition works, but in this case instead of a television set, invisible intuitive information comes through a "human antenna" and manifests through different "human channels."

what are some of the channels of intuition?

Although intuition can come through a multitude of different channels, here are a few channels widely agreed upon as being the most common:

1. **Feeling:** This intuitive channel has to do with perceiving, or feeling, information in your body. For example, it can be a "gut feeling," feeling tightness in the throat when around someone who is holding back tears, or feeling a tingling in your feet when you're on the right track about something.

2. **Hearing:** Some people experience intuitive information via inner words and sounds. For example, one child says, "I'm thinking of a number between one and ten—which is it?" and the other child internally hears the answer "three," tipping him off to the correct answer. Please note how this sensation differs from the "hearing voices" that can be a symptom of psychosis. For example, a person who hears a voice advising doing harm to self or others is a red flag that requires immediate professional help.

3. **Seeing:** Intuitive information in this channel is perceived through inner visual pictures. Using the previous example involving the guessing of numbers, another child sees the number three pop up as if on the movie screen of the mind.

Intuitive data can be as simple as providing answers to a guessing game or as complex as premonitions about the future. The perception of thoughts or feelings in a room, of current world events, or even of meteorological or geological events can all be part of the intuitive channel as well.

availability of information

We are all intuitive and empathic, and we all have the ability to cultivate these inborn abilities to greater levels through use, intentional practice, and study. Highly intuitive children are born with these abilities already working at high capacity with no training. This is not to say that their access to these channels yields perfect results. But it does suggest a likelihood of experiencing some heightened degree of input on one or more of these channels.

Now I want to use a more up-to-date television analogy—cable television. Highly intuitive people are different from other people in that there are more channels open and thus more information available. A basic cable package gets you the main available stations, which is similar to the large majority of people who mostly work from information provided by their five senses in life and are also using their intuition and empathy to some degree. Highly intuitive children are born not only with the basic package of the main senses but, as an added bonus, they have a free, built-in installation of the premium cable channels. These premium cable channels give them access to quite a bit more data. In particular, these children may have crystal-clear reception of "the family channel," "the peer and classroom channel," and "the world channel." This last channel pulls in signals registering from all around the world. On some days, they can pick up a signal about something going on in China, and on another day the signal may originate from Ecuador or Russia.

It may sound enticing that these kids are born with the extra cable package, and it can be rewarding when they learn the operating instructions, but life can be complicated and stressful when they don't know how to shut off some of the channels. Imagine yourself as a child innocently playing in the yard when all of a sudden the Chinese channel goes off, alerting you to some kind of mass danger in China. Disturbing? You bet. These children didn't ask for the download of information; it just happened.

When you understand that your child might be tuning in to different channels, you can use your own detective skills to see which channel he or she might be on and help your child tune it out. Here are some clues and examples that indicate the major channels:

The Family Channel

- ★ picking up on unspoken feelings among family members
- ★ sensing that a relative in another part of the country is sick before the illness is detected or announced
- ★ tuning in to a parent's worry, headache, or stress
- ★ picking up information within the closest circle of the child's important people

The Peer and Classroom Channel

- ★ picking up on the feelings of classmates or a teacher
- ★ expressing unspoken tensions in the classroom through their own behavior (for example, a burst of anger)
- ★ feeling unspoken class problems; somaticizing the pain
- ★ thinking strongly about one classmate or friend for no particular reason, only to learn later that this person was experiencing a great difficulty (or, more welcome, a happy event)

The World Channel

- ★ a sudden thought about problems in another part of the world, accompanied by a sense of urgency, unrest, and unbalance
- ★ a sense of compassion and humanitarianism, sometimes accompanied by existential worry
- ★ a general feeling of being ill at ease with the state of the earth
- ★ a strong feeling of urgency about people, places, and events that are foreign and unfamiliar

As an adult you can tailor your support of the child, listening for specific clues. Intuitive children easily leap to general conclusions, so it is helpful to break down their images or feelings into small, specific details. Let me give you an example of how this might work.

❋ Kyle — age 7

Practical Help for a Child Troubled by the World Channel

Kyle was an inquisitive boy about to enter second grade. He was having a great summer with his friends when all of a sudden one day he woke up in a pretty dark mood that he just couldn't shake. His parents wracked their brains trying to figure out what it might be. Things were going well at home and with his peers, and there had been no new physical ailments or unusually stressful situations in the past few weeks. Even his diet and exercise were right on track. After hours of moping around, crying, and telling his parents, "I'm just so sad and I don't know why. Leave me alone!" he suddenly, intently, wanted to do something for Africa; his heart and mind were locked on this country. At first his parents were puzzled. As far as they were aware, Kyle had not seen or read anything about Africa that was scary or traumatic. Kyle told them his feeling had nothing to do with anything he could remember seeing.

His parents helped him in a couple of different ways. They listened to him, without interruption, as he spoke about his feelings about Africa. As Kyle spoke, it became clear he was deeply concerned about the plight of the animals there, especially the gorillas. To honor his concerns, his parents helped him search for an organization working to protect gorillas, and they made a donation. In the following days, Kyle's mood transformed dramatically because he was able to do something to help. Interestingly, a few weeks later, the same African gorillas Kyle had been worrying about appeared on the cover of a major news magazine. There had been a recent surge in poaching in Congo, and the gorillas were indeed in trouble. Young Kyle apparently tuned into it before it hit the national press.

Kyle's antenna reached all the way to Africa. He could feel the problem before he could explain it. Eventually the information floated up to the surface of his awareness, which gave both Kyle and his parents the clues they needed to take some action. He was able to put his natural humanitarianism to work and calm down his emotions. In doing so, I think he also pulled his focus—or his antenna, if you will—in closer to his day-to-day reality. When his parents demonstrated they could take an action in response to his concerns, it increased his sense of mastery over a seemingly unsolvable problem. It also helped break down the far-reaching intuitive information into a more meaningful reality that he could relate to as a child.

Kyle's story is an example of the skill of regulating the intuitive antenna. The specific steps that were used in helping Kyle bring his awareness from the global channel back to home included the following:

* **Attending to the initial upset and helping the child calm down:** Providing immediate comfort and attentive soothing.

* **Listening for evidence of the intuitive channel; determining from which channel the information is arriving:** Kyle's parents didn't initially know what the big upset was all about—the answer emerged when Kyle started to give details and they could listen for how far the channel reached.

* **Identifying the particular concern:** Kyle was worried about the gorillas in Africa.

* **Tailoring your parenting response to the specific concern:** Kyle needed help addressing his specific concerns once they emerged clearly (although these types of concerns are not always so clear).

* **Breaking it down into a meaningful, child-friendly reality:** Researching organizations that help the gorillas in Africa.

* **Making it tangible and taking action, if needed:** Making the donation empowered Kyle because he could do something to help.

Intuitive Children Tuning in to the Pain of the World

The day after 9/11, I was at my daughter's preschool when I had a striking lesson of how intuitive children can experience the world channel. I remember feeling comforted by the familiarity of the little red schoolhouse and the simplicity of watching a group of 3-year-olds engage in their usual play. They were painting, running after chickens, and climbing over the play structure. It was a peaceful respite from thinking about the atrocities of the preceding morning. But my bubble soon burst. As I observed the children playing, I started to see a couple of children acting out the collapse of the Twin Towers. One little boy kept building huge towers of blocks and smashing them down with toy airplanes; another drew buildings on fire with airplanes crashing into them. I asked the parents of these children if, to their knowledge, their kids had seen the planes and towers on television, or maybe heard about them. They emphatically answered, "No." They were shocked that their children were acting out what happened 3,000 miles away. Some of the parents were also distraught, remembering that for several days preceding the attacks, their children had been inconsolable. No matter what they did, they were at a loss as to the cause or cure for their children's discomfort.

The trauma of the 9/11 events made me forget having seen a drawing of an airplane flying into a flaming building. It had been done by a 3-year-old—*before* the attacks occurred. I am still amazed by the effects on the psyches of America's children, although not all were impacted to the same degree. I learned that some well-meaning parents had left their televisions on, exposing their children to the repeated images of the Twin Towers falling—and yet these children were not upset. The child who drew the plane and burning building was unusually upset the day *before* the attack. Her mom tried to soothe her; the child was too young to learn about the nature of the attacks so her mom couldn't teach her about how to avoid taking on the pain of the world. Instead, she helped her daughter quiet herself by spending time in nature, extra time snuggling together, and by trying to remain as calm as possible herself. It was a rough couple of weeks, but the child moved through it with no lasting harm.

Intuitive children sometimes tune in to global conditions; if we lived in a perfect world, this wouldn't be a problem—but we don't. I'm struck by the depth of empathy in children who tune in to the world channel. I see the seeds of humanitarianism in this kind of empathy, but it can also feel like a burden to come into this awareness so soon. For children with this level of awareness and sensitivity, it is important not to overload them with the problems of the world. They often feel them already. It is helpful to keep a finger on the pulse of these children as they enter school to see if they are feeling overburdened by what they are learning about the world's problems. Unlike children who quite naturally feel less empathy and may need quite a bit of exposure to stories that increase their empathy for the world and other people, with the highly intuitive child, a little exposure tends to go a long way. Some curricula, in seeking to educate children and teach empathy, may backfire on highly intuitive, empathic children who may feel despair over the condition of the world. The aperture of empathy and feeling in these children is open so wide that they can be quite vulnerable to excessive exposure to the world's problems.

I recommend that parents and teachers keep an eye out for signs of stress caused by exposure to painful stories, particularly if solutions aren't part of the discussion. It can be anxiety provoking for kids to learn about crises without empowering them to make a difference. Working toward solutions, as in Kyle's case, helps to foster a sense of hope, meaning, and empowerment. The next chapter further explores how stress can manifest in multidimensional ways for an intuitive child and how to reduce its impact.

stress and the
intuitive child

Reality is the leading cause of stress
among those in touch with it.

Lily Tomlin

Your Stress Is My Stress

In this chapter, we build on understanding the intuitive child by first taking a closer look at the physical and empathic side of what these children experience. When an intuitive, empathic child encounters a person with significant stress, the child often automatically mirrors, or matches, the feeling in the other person, creating a your-stress-is-my-stress syndrome. The pressure of "your stress is my stress" results in children routinely dealing with much more than what should be on their own emotional plate. No one deserves to have more than his own share of stress. Unfortunately, the intuitive child innocently carries more than a personal load. Finely tuned into others, their turbocharged "antenna" picks up more signals than do most people's. Too much stress compromises a person's health, thinking, and emotional life, so it is worth actively helping to reduce these risks in our children. To help intuitive kids reduce their stress levels, we must effectively identify the causes.

Have you ever been in a bad mood and noticed that your child seemed to catch your mood, as if it were a cold? These children are exquisitely sensitive to the moods of others, especially their parents. Why is this? Recent advances in neuroscience may suggest clues for answering such questions and may help shed light on the biological reasons for unusually empathic reactions to stress.

Intuitive Empathy and Social Neuroscience Discoveries

In the 1990s, empathy made it onto the map of brain research. In 1992, at the University of Parma in Italy, Giacomo Rizzolatti discovered an unusual group of cells in the brains of monkeys that he called mirror neurons. He found these neurons firing in concert with mimicry (with what was being seen)—as opposed to actual performance—thus "mirroring" the actions, and perhaps emotions, of others. He called this group of brain cells the mirror neuron system (MNS).

Rizzolatti discovered the MNS purely by chance. On a hot day in Parma, Italy, one of his research assistants walked into the laboratory with an ice cream cone. A research monkey, after observing the assistant licking the ice cream cone, copied the motions, as if licking an ice cream cone himself. Rizzolatti and his associates recorded specific sensorimotor activity during this mimicking behavior. Because the recorded increase in neuronal activity occurred simultaneously with the mirroring behavior, he named these cells a mirror neuron system.[1]

It is now postulated that MNS activity could be associated with communication and empathy between humans. In his book *Social Intelligence: The Revolutionary New Science of Human Relationships*, psychologist and bestselling author Daniel Goleman explains that "mirror neurons make emotions contagious, letting the feelings we witness flow through us, helping us get in sync and follow what's going on. We 'feel' the other in the broadest sense of the word: sensing their sentiments, their movements, their sensations, their emotions as they act inside us. Social skills depend on mirror neurons."[2] This could help explain why some children catch another's mood as easily as they catch colds. After identification of the MNS in animals, social neuroscientists have taken their research in directions that may help us understand the basis for varying degrees of empathy.

Christian Keysers, PhD, at the University of Groningen in the Netherlands, is looking at how mirror neurons impact a continuum of empathy behaviors. Dr. Keysers' work, which has received the prestigious European Union Marie Curie Excellence Award, may demonstrate why some individuals seem to have turbocharged empathic abilities: Preliminary results indicate a possible correlation between high scorers on an empathy scale and higher levels of mirror neuron activity. He states, "How empathic we are seems to be related to how strongly our mirror neuron system is activated."[3] I am curious to see how such research will inform our understanding of children with highly active MNS areas as well as those with a low-firing MNS.

Highly intuitive, empathic children may need to learn how to quiet their heightened responses to people and environmental stimuli by learning how to regulate the "volume" of these channels and calm down. In many ways, the skills taught in this book teach how to regulate and manage the overabundance of data that may be the result of living under the high end of the MNS bell curve. My goal isn't to get these kids into the average range, but rather to help them feel more comfortable with their unusually active brains. As we teach children to be more comfortable with finely tuned, responsive systems, we help them to adapt their particular biology to the tasks of living. If we don't help them learn how to modulate their sometimes extreme responses to the amount of data they are exposed to, the result will be more stress on the child.

The Intuitive Child under Stress

Stress plays a fascinating role in the lives of humans. Too little stress and we fall into boredom, poorly engaged with our lives and the world around us. Too much stress and the brain starts to sputter and shut down its peak efficiency. Just the right amount of stress creates the ideal blend of being awake and alert without the damaging chemical interactions that occur at higher stress levels in the body.

Intuitive children might experience more stress than meets the eye. If you have a child who has the ability to inadvertently tune in to unspoken conflicts among family members, classmates, or friends, the child will be encountering more than his fair share of potential stressors.

How to Spot Stress in an Intuitive Child

In the interest of trying to keep your child's stress levels manageable, it can be helpful to know how to spot some of the ways that stress will show up in an intuitive child.

- ★ **An implosion of emotion** resulting in a system shutdown when too much input comes in all at once. This is also known as *acting in* with stress. The child becomes more sullen and perhaps jumps quickly to the conclusion that far too many problems are his fault. Children have their own personal styles when it comes to stress, but environment can also play a factor. If the message in the family is to keep your emotions quiet or "I don't want to hear any more about your crazy intuitions or ideas," then the child is far more likely to stuff his feelings and *act in* with the stress. Taken to the extreme, this reaction to stress can begin to depress the child and even result in self-injuring behaviors.

- ★ **A sudden burst or explosion of emotion** as the child tries to shake off all the stress she has pulled in from other people and environments—also known as *acting out* the stress. This can show up as a burst of anger as the child expresses her feelings for having taken on too many pressures from other people or simply as a knee-jerk way to get some space from others.

- ★ **Inexplicable emotions:** "I'm feeling 'X' and I don't know why and I can't get rid of it!" This reaction usually happens when a child has taken on a specific negative emotion from someone else, as if by contagion. The child may have moved away from the situation, but the negative feeling can still linger if he "took it on."

- ★ **Psychosomaticizing:** The emotional states that have been absorbed turn into actual physical pain. Usually these physical problems can't be corroborated with a medical diagnosis and can leave adults wondering if the child is making up her symptoms. Look for unexplained headaches and stomachaches, or other migrating aches and pains. (We'll cover psychosomaticizing in more depth in Chapter 5.)

★ **Social hypervigilance:** The child might begin to imagine that he is seeing problems where there are none. The child might start to draw conclusions about people and events that are off the mark. The hypervigilance is also an attempt to control intuitive surprises that don't feel good; the child adopts this behavior as a self-protection mechanism.

★ **Anxiety:** The anxiety might be the result of having worrisome premonitions, intuitions, or worrisome exchanges with other people that they feel they can't control. High stress levels are also a precursor to anxiety symptoms, which is yet another reason for proactive stress management.

★ **Clouded decision-making ability:** Intuitives under stress can lose their center like anyone else. Because intuitive, empathic children so naturally tune in to the needs and desires of others, they can start to pay more attention to other people's opinions in lieu of their own. This clouds decision making. They may also deliberately not honor what they authentically want, opting instead for the choice that makes other people happy.

★ **Distractibility:** The child may have difficulty focusing because she is picking up on too many emotional and intuitive signals in the environment.

★ **Spaciness:** Intuitive children sometimes are referred to as having their heads in the clouds. Maybe they are lost in their own interesting thoughts about the nature of the universe or are watching their minds leap to an intuitive conclusion on a problem they've been trying to solve. Or maybe they are merely taking a break from sensory input.

⭑ **Depression:** Sometimes children will reach a state of feeling that there is nothing they can do to exert more control over the stressors they are encountering, and this loss of control can rob them of energy. Feelings of isolation, waning meaning in life, and feeling like their abilities are a curse can all contribute to depression. If a child is judged, ridiculed, or shamed for his abilities, it can lead to feelings of depression.

⭑ **Exhaustion:** The child may run out of steam from working too hard to rebalance her system on a regular basis. For example, the bustle of school or the mall might energize many children but leave the intuitive child totally drained. When an intuitive child exercises her sensate abilities to an extreme level, say in a very sensate teacher's classroom, it can also create fatigue in a child. Persistent stress, nervous system overload, and anxiety also contribute to exhaustion.

Trouble Asking for Help

The same amazing empathy that gives an intuitive child the ability to tune in to others and instinctively know what they need can also sabotage the child when it comes to managing his own stress levels. For example, when intuitive children detect, or perceive, that expressing their stress is going to cause upset around them, they are less likely to freely and honestly express it. Most intuitive children are keenly aware of wanting to avoid the double trouble of dealing with the original problem and the potential upset in other people when they express their own stress or need.

Intuitive children might need even *more* permission to express what is bothering them and to be reminded that it is not their job to take care of other people's feelings. They also need to hear that their feelings are welcome within the family, even when it seems like these feelings could be uncomfortable for parents to hear. Although it might seem obvious to point this out, intuitive children might relax and open up when they are reminded that it is not their job to take on other people's problems.

How Collective Attitudes about Intuition Impact Children's Stress Levels

How people feel collectively about intuition can contribute to intuitive children's stress. During the Dark ages in Western Europe there was terrible persecution and fear related to intuitive gifts. Witches were burned, intuitive gifts were judged as the work of the devil, and countless women were tortured for their sixth sense and healing abilities. Fear of intuition ran rampant and people learned to keep their intuitions secret at the risk of death.

Today we are gaining more acceptance of intuition in our personal lives, at home, in business, and at every place in between. I personally experienced this opening of intuitive acceptance in my own family system when I was at my paternal grandmother's deathbed. Just before she died, she gave me an interesting message. It was one of the last things she ever coherently said to me. She said, "It is safe now to use the gift." I knew exactly what she meant, and I thought it was beautiful that some of her parting words were ones of freedom to use intuitive gifts in life.

The collective attitude shift is great news for intuitive children and adults. It is finally safe to talk about this topic and investigate what it means to genuinely give these children what they need when they need it and not give them a childhood they have to recover from in adulthood. The growing sense of it being safe to talk about intuition means that this acceptance can trickle down into families, schools, community organizations, and all the places that touch the lives of our children. Intuitive children can sense this openness and it truly contributes to their sense of feeling safe to be themselves in the world.

We further contribute to a sense of safety for intuitive children by being there to listen to their experiences in a down-to-earth, accepting style. This style leaves plenty of room for curiosity about the child's experience—even when it is remarkably different, as many intuitive children's experiences prove to be. A down-to-earth approach toward children's intuition doesn't inflate or deflate their experience. Intuition can be inflated by responses that demonstrate, "Wow, I think you are extra special, because you have *this* intuition." I'll be the first to admit that it is tempting to drop my jaw when I experience striking intuitive insights from a child, especially when they are right on target, such as a prediction. But I work very hard not to do just that. Intuitive kids are quite perceptive, and if they detect they have your undivided attention when they share this part of themselves and they see that now they are finally special in your eyes, they can start to link this impression to their self-worth. These children are then at risk of overexerting this part of themselves to garner the adoration of the adult mirror in their life. Worse still, the intuitive child might think this trait is the only thing the parent wants to see and is the reason for being loved.

Children need to know that they are loved simply for being themselves, not for what they do or for a special ability. The child could be the equivalent of an Olympic medalist in intuition, but it is still important for the child to receive the message that "I love you just for who you are." These messages are especially important to seed in those ordinary moments when you are just hanging out together, the moments of just being. I know of no greater gift that can be given to children than their knowing they are loved and accepted just for being themselves. It is like bedrock for the personality, like a deep well to drink from and a gift that no one can take away.

Children are deflated in their intuitive reality every time we judge, deny, or pull away from what they are sharing. When children sense that the content of what they are sharing is not permissible, they rein it in. Unfortunately, they may also be reining in their life-force energy and cutting off from a part of themselves. The meta-message the child receives in such instances is that it is not safe to fully be themselves.

I think adults are at risk of unconsciously responding in an inflating or deflating way to children's intuition until they have come to a sense of peace and acceptance that the gift is just another part of life. When we can treat it as something as natural as any other human ability, it loses the polarizing charges of extraordinarily special or terrifyingly weird. Both of these extremes are risky for an intuitive child.

Most of us grow up in families in which we receive some kind of message about intuition and these messages can linger long into our adult lives. If you grew up in a home where intuition was accepted as a means of trusting yourself and finding your true north, this is a gift. I love to hear stories of people who grew up in homes where intuition was valued and spoken of readily. If you received conflicting messages about your intuition as a child, it might be helpful to reflect on what those messages were and to consciously choose the beliefs you would like to hold now.

Here are a few classics that shut down intuition in a family:

★ "We are a rational family. We only believe what we can see and prove."

★ "You are forbidden to speak of intuitions outside of our home."

★ "That's crazy"—from parents scared of hearing a prediction.

★ "That's all in your imagination"—from dismissive parents.

★ Such talk is "the work of the devil."

★ "People are going to think you are weird, crazy, or psychotic."

★ "You are going to scare everyone away," or "There is no way for you to know these things"—from parents who are very frightened of the child's ability

★ "Never speak of something like that again"—from parents who do not know how to guide their child concerning when it is appropriate and when it is inappropriate to share their intuitive impressions (for example, telling the neighbor of an impending hardship) and opting for a global rule instead.

Social Stress for Intuitive Children

Although all children experience some social stress at certain times in their lives, highly intuitive children are often faced with unique challenges in this area. The following story takes you straight into the world of an intuitive teen at school.

❋ Tonya — age 13

Navigating a Junior-High Conflict as a Highly Intuitive Young Teen

When I met her, Tonya was in junior high school and experiencing all the stressors that come with a changing body and peer relationships at this stage of life. Tonya was bright and capable academically, although she was showing signs of wanting to "dumb down" at school to avoid the stress of her peers noticing that she didn't quite fit in. Secretly she felt like an outsider. She was bored with the academics but totally stressed by what she was feeling emotionally. Her junior high was a large, bustling city school that required changing classrooms between periods. She hated moving through the sea of students. Part of what made it so hard was that she found it unsettling to pick up on so many people's feelings when she walked from class to class. The din of voices in the hall was a cacophony of noise to her and it often gave her a headache, a stomachache, or both.

On this particular day, she had a hunch that something bad was going to happen at lunch. Her feelings weren't clear enough today to give her something more direct. "How irritating," she thought to herself, "to have this random feeling of something bad coming up in a couple of hours. Ridiculous." She needed to focus on her afternoon math test, so she tried to put it out of her head. The test came and went. She was a bit more distracted than usual during the test and felt pretty tired. Then lunchtime came and, sure enough, one of her friends launched at her with anger for something that was a complete misunderstanding. She was stunned by the unexpected force of her friend's anger and, though she didn't feel at fault, started to absorb the friend's anger into her own body. She started to feel lousy, guilty over nothing, and ran the whole thing over and over in her head for the rest of the afternoon.

Tonya's conflict at school is a good example of how empathic stress can hit below the skin and linger longer than for other personality types that are not as affected. She felt an impending sense of something difficult coming up (maybe she was even intuiting the feelings of someone being angry with her), she took the anger into her body (empathic absorption), and she struggled with trying to shake it off. Tonya was having a stress response related to having a teenage conflict with a friend, which was further complicated by her being an intuitive.

Fortunately, Tonya had a wonderful teacher at her school that genuinely seemed to "get" her. Tonya spent a few minutes with her teacher, explaining what was going on, and she immediately started to feel better because she could express herself without fearing judgment from this adult. After Tonya was visibly more collected within herself, the teacher offered to help the teens with a conflict resolution session so they could work out the conflict. At first, Tonya's anxiety increased, but she agreed because she felt so safe with this teacher. After school, the girls met with the teacher and they worked the conflict out to a place where both girls felt reconnected as friends. Tonya experienced tremendous relief and felt a sense of accomplishment that she could get through such an uncomfortable scene. The knot in her stomach cleared up almost immediately and she took a sigh of relief. She felt like she was back to her old self again.

What happens when a child is in a chronically stressful situation, be it family stress or how the child is responding to a teacher or school? Of course, this issue affects all children regardless of their capacities for intuition or empathy because all children deserve to experience safety and environments that support their growth and development. We may need to pay extra attention to our young people who possess heightened receptors for the stressors of life, though. We can provide them with the skills to manage their stress levels so they aren't dealing with chronic taxing of the brain's fine balancing systems. Ultimately, when we help them learn their own unique language for managing stress, we are also helping them to feel comfortable in their own skin.

The Stress of Feeling Different

One of the issues that can contribute to the stress experienced by intuitive children is feeling out of place socially. I often hear these children complain about feeling different from their peers. Seven-year-old Tracy repeatedly came home from school complaining to her mom, "I feel so different, Mommy. Why can't I find any friends who are more like me? Maybe you can find me a school that is more spiritual. Maybe I'll find kids who are more like me there." Up until her seventh year, Tracy was able to freely talk about her intuitions in the guise of imaginary play with her friends.

When children are naturally living in the world of make-believe play, it is easy to slip into multidimensional realities as another extension or expression of this reality. For the highly intuitive child, it also serves as a doorway to perceiving an unseen reality (intuitive information) of which others are unaware. But when children start to develop more logical and concrete ways of thinking at approximately age 7, this change can leave some intuitive children in a bit of a shock socially. Suddenly their friends may wonder why they are still engaging in "babyish" imaginary play. Intuitive children themselves may wonder why they haven't moved on from that behavior. The empathic child registers this perception and feels different from the rest of the class or peer group. Highly intuitive children experience the leap into more logical processing that is associated with concrete operations just like the rest of their peers, but they may experience stress in having their intuitive insights suddenly highlighted because they can't be hidden in the guise of imaginary play as easily. In a desire to fit in and be successful, the child might start to rein in socially and attempt to hide his intuitive insights. If you notice this change happening in your child, stay alert to finding places, peers, and other adults who offer the child a place where his authentic nature is welcomed and valued. Listen to what your child is asking you for.

✷ Tracy — age 7

Expressing Her Needs to Find Like-Minded Intuitive Children and Acceptance

Tracy gave her mom clues that she wanted to be with others who were more like her and to be in an environment where she could feel at home. Tracy's mom responded by increasing her daughter's time with some other intuitive children the family knew outside of the school and by spending time occasionally at a spiritual community where the child felt particularly happy and alive. Tracy grew to trust that she could ask her mom for more of these contacts when she felt the need arise. Astutely, Tracy even remarked to her mom one day that she worried she would lose her "spirit self" if she didn't have enough play-dates with friends who were "more like her" and have hang-out time at the special place in the woods where she felt so alive and safe. This remark certainly got her mom's attention, and she honored it by taking her daughter seriously.

What does Tracy's story tell us about children who feel outside of the norm when all children of this age are naturally moving into the world of realistic, concrete operations? Tracy was making this developmental leap, too, but her growth was asynchronous from that of her peers. For one thing, she possessed the self-reflective capacity to comment that she was worried that she might lose her connection to her spirit self—a highly unusual comment for a 7-year-old. Tracy was a typical 7-year-old in so many ways, but far ahead of her years in others.

The Importance of Safety in Helping Intuitive Children Manage Stress

One of the most important gifts we can give intuitive children is to let them know it is safe and acceptable for them to express themselves fully with us—even when these expressions might include unusual intuitive insights. When an adult judges, rejects, shames, or denies a child's intuition, they are doing the same to the heart and soul of the child. We can shut down or repress children's intuition by not honoring it, but it goes even further than this psychologically. Because intuition and empathy are hardwired traits, they are integral components of the self. When children receive the message that intuition and empathy are bad, they are inclined to deny or hide these important parts of themselves. I say "inclined" because no matter how much children try to suppress their true nature or be who the parent, teacher, or society wants them to be, they can never completely squelch this essential, authentic nature.

I often see evidence of the strength of the traits of high intuition and empathy in my adult psychotherapy clients, many of whom, despite childhoods where they received intense criticism and strong messages to hide these parts of themselves, are capable of reclaiming and utilizing their abilities with the support that I'll talk about in Chapter 11.

True safety is also created within a loving bond where the child feels securely attached to the parent. In an attached parenting bond, children from their first days of life learn that their caregivers are deeply in tune to their needs and will be there for them. If the child cries, he will be held. If the child is hungry, he will be fed. The child learns that he can trust other people and it is safe to need and have those needs met. This attuned style of parenting supports the foundation for most everything that I cover in this book. It is like money in the emotional bank of life for your child, with dividends paid out not only in future relationships, but in overall well-being and resiliency to life's challenges as well.

When children don't feel safe, anxiety levels rise and we see children overcompensating by acting out, acting in, or just plain overworking to try to manage their environment and their own inner feeling state. A lack of feeling safe breeds reactivity, a disconnection from one's own wisdom, and tightens the mind, body, and heart.

The Value of Meditation in Calming Children's Stress Levels

Meditation is a terrific practice for children who need additional help in managing stress levels. Once considered a fringe spiritual practice in the West, many neuroscientists have come to understand and widely document the proven value of meditation's health benefits on the body and mind.[4]

Meditation can be a wonderful stress management tool for intuitive children for many reasons. I personally can speak for the value of meditation as an intuitive empath based on my twenty-year meditation practice. Meditation centers my mind, calms my nervous system, brings me more fully into the present moment, and gets me out of my head and connected to my heart and spirit.

Part of the trick of introducing meditation to children is finding a way to present it that doesn't turn them off. At first, it might feel strange, slow, or foreign for the child to close his eyes and do a simple breathing meditation. Our fast-paced culture runs counter to the slower pace of meditation. It might be helpful to remember that there are other ways to become quiet and to relax. The simple act of climbing into a tree and looking out on nature below can be a wonderful meditation. And for small children who can naturally find their *flow state* in play, art, or imaginary musings, the thought of sitting down to follow the breath might be developmentally inappropriate. However, if a child can sit still in school for at least five minutes, he can probably take five minutes to practice a simple meditation exercise.

One of the easiest ways to begin teaching your child meditation is by paying attention to the in-and-out movements of the breath. When the child's mind wanders from the breath, she should gently return to it. Based on what feels best, the child can close her eyes and sit comfortably or lie down. I recommend that you or another trusted adult be present during this experience to create a loving, meditative space for your child. Since your child is intuitive, she will be able to sense the calm and peaceful feeling being generated from your own meditation alongside her own.

Other simple forms of meditation for children include mentally repeating or singing a single word or phrase such as "peace," "beauty," "happy," or "I am free." You can work with your child to determine what words help him to feel calm.

Review of Calming the Intuitive Child's Stress

★ Listen to the child without judgment and without inflating or deflating.

★ Stay calm and try not to match the child's fear or stress.

★ Give permission for the child to express her feelings.

★ Evaluate for sensory overload, and help to reduce sensory inputs.

★ Take some deep breaths together.

★ Clear conflicts if necessary.

★ If the child is caught in a random intuition, help to release it.

★ Practice asking, "Is this mine?"

★ Look for ways to shift gears and orient to the present moment.

when an intuitive child
needs professional help

Something opens our wings.
Something makes boredom and hurt disappear.
Someone fills the cup in front of us...

RUMI

When an intuitive child is experiencing high stress that doesn't decrease despite parental interventions, it may be time to seek the help of a qualified professional. You, your child, and your family need not carry this burden on your own. Well-timed therapeutic support for a child can change not only his life for the better, but yours as well.

This chapter focuses on a few of the more common times when an intuitive child might benefit from therapy, as well as dealing with some of the questions that arise when intuition is confused with a psychiatric diagnosis. I've chosen to focus on anxiety, depression, attention deficit disorder (ADD), sensory processing disorder, and trauma. In particular, the focus will be on how significant intuition and empathy levels can affect and complicate these diagnoses or confuse people by appearing to be a common psychiatric diagnosis when that might not be the case.

Intuition can coexist with any diagnosis and its presence can magnify those conditions in some unique ways. However, it is not a diagnosis in itself, nor is it a psychological pathology. This chapter will help you sort through the question of when to get extra help for your child. It is certainly not a complete profile of when you might need help; it is only a sampling of what I've seen as common problem areas over the years in my practice as a therapist. Professional help may be called for in other arenas as well, particularly related to physical support for highly sensitive bodies. Those instances will be addressed in Chapter 5.

Anxiety

Anxiety in children is an emotional condition that can be complicated by high intuition. Highly intuitive children sort through quite a bit of additional data about people, places, and events, and sometimes the information they encounter is threatening and can trigger anxiety symptoms, such as hypervigilance, fear, worry, sleep disturbance or nightmares, somatic distress, and difficulty relaxing. As you may recall from Chapter 2, these upsets might stem from sensing world dangers, ecological instability, or even trouble brewing on the street. This unsettling information can disrupt the child's inner sense of safety, spike stress levels, and put them at risk for anxiety.

Two additional factors impact children who experience problems with anxiety: stress triggers and biological inheritance. Stress overload raises the likelihood of anxiety symptoms. In many cases, stress is the precipitating factor that triggers anxiety in sensitive children.[1] The good news is that staying committed to stress management can greatly reduce the likelihood of emergent anxiety.

We also know that there is a genetic component to anxiety. This component has been identified in research studies of infants as young as 6 months of age.[2] Sometimes referred to as *biological sensitivity,* this component is associated with a child's genetically determined temperament. Again, the good news in this research is that well-attuned parenting to a child's needs greatly reduces the triggers for anxiety from infancy on up.

Carl Jung believed that a child's anxiety is associated with the unconscious life of the parent.[3] In other words, if you as a parent have a significant unhealed fear or trauma, it is possible that your child will be affected by this fear. I would add that intuitive children might be especially attuned to the responses that parents and caregivers have to the worries of the child. If the child detects the adult recoiling in fear when a worry is communicated, the child will notice the response. Layering our own worry on top of a vulnerable child's worry sometimes adds more fuel to the fire. By contrast, providing a calm, steady presence while they move through the fear will be a terrific help. Staying calm and centered when a child is losing control over a big fear is not an easy thing to do. Empathic parents can be especially vulnerable to matching or mirroring the child's worried state. It may be helpful to remember to take a breath and take a step back from the situation. The peaceful witnessing you bring to your child's worries can be a powerful healing tool for your child.

combating worries with an internal feeling of safety

Children naturally learn to anchor their sense of safety through the key relationships in their lives, and it is natural for a child to look outside of himself to see, feel, and detect safety. Unfortunately, tuning in to outside relationships and events can backfire on highly intuitive children. Because intuitive, empathic children are so adept at tuning in to other people and events, it is easy to start to pick up and assimilate external worries, fears, and dangers. This is another manifestation of the your-stress-is-my-stress experience discussed in Chapter 3.

One way to work with this tendency is to cultivate the concept that safety is a feeling that exists within. The more open a child's intuitive, empathic aperture, the bigger the need to have a way to connect with a sense of inner peace and safety. Needing the world to be perfectly safe in order to feel internally safe is out of reach. But focusing on inner peace and well-being redirects the mind away from the worrisome triggers out in the world and builds a sense of safety. Best of all, this inner feeling of safety can comfort the highly intuitive child no matter how lousy things may feel out in the world.

It is natural for children to feel some fear from time to time as a result of the intuitive information they come across, but hopefully this fear can be resolved with appropriate parental support. If this is not the case, and your child is experiencing worry and fear that impede her ability to enjoy life and thrive, it may be time to get professional help for the anxiety. Anxiety can persist throughout life; learning how to manage it with the assistance of a skilled therapist who specializes in anxiety is a wonderful gift to give an anxious child.

Depression

Depression is a growing problem in the lives of children in the United States, affecting one in eight teens and one in thirty-three children. Suicide rates have doubled for youth in the last generation (1979–1998), making it the third-leading cause of death of 15- to 24-year-olds.[4] These numbers are food for thought for all of us within this culture and a call for help for today's youth.

According to Elaine N. Aron, PhD, author of *The Highly Sensitive Child* and *The Highly Sensitive Person*, "I discovered several studies that report that intuitive types are the most likely to have suicidal thoughts when they are depressed. This makes great sense—intuitive types tend to take things to their full conclusion, often without knowing the steps of reasoning that got them there. Highly sensitive people are often intuitive types, hence when they begin to think about themselves or the state of their relationships or the state of the world, or all three at once, they can often come to very dark conclusions."[5] Dr. Aron raises specific concerns that address the importance of listening and staying attuned to the needs of intuitive people when they are depressed. I agree with the importance of paying close attention to the nature of their intuitive conclusions.

The same wonderful quality of seeing the big picture in life, feeling the gestalt of a situation, and quickly jumping to places of intuitive discovery and insight can backfire, leading to impulsive or irrational decisions in a depressed intuitive individual of any age. Skilled intervention is important when the child comes to overwhelming, harmful, and irrational conclusions about his own life and the world.

What are some of the things that contribute to depression in an intuitive, empathic child? The reasons include being overwhelmed by too much painful input from their immediate life or the world, exhaustion from overworking their empathic abilities, untreated anxiety, a loss of self that comes from pleasing others at the expense of one's own needs and wants, and a feeling that they are not at home in this world.

Depression in intuitives shares an interesting relationship with spiritual hunger in both children and adults. Spiritual hunger whispers to us when we lose our sense of inspiration, and it roars with the demand to live a more purposeful life when we drift off track. Perhaps spiritual hunger can even set off episodes of clinical depression, especially if there is a genetic propensity or vulnerability. When I listen for what a person's spirit is hungry for, I often detect a hunger for something deeper in life. Dr. Aron believes that one of the most important ways we can prevent this kind of intuitive depression is by ensuring that the child has a deep sense of meaning in her life.[6]

With an eye to preventing this form of depression, it makes good sense to pay attention to whether or not children feel a sense of meaning in their lives. Do they feel like they matter and that their lives make a difference? Children and teens are every bit as capable as adults of considering and struggling with questions of life's meaning—even to the point of agonizing over the big existential questions.

Whether or not your child is wrestling with life's big questions, I recommend keeping an ear tuned for requests for help, and also being proactive in supporting a child's inquiries into the meaning of his life. We can do this by valuing and validating their unique insights, by reassuring them that they absolutely have a life purpose and that they can take their time in the unfolding of this purpose (intuitive kids often want to rush their purpose), and by reminding them of how much they are valued simply for being themselves.

Questions such as "Who am I?" "Why is there so much pain and suffering in the world?" "Why am I me, and you are you?" and even, "I want to help other people and the world, but I'm just a little kid and how can I make a difference now?" are all some of the basic questions heard from children who are wrestling with meaning. These questions and struggles are real and vital for their development. While tangling with questions of meaning can be downright bumpy at times, intuitive children largely move through them when given plenty of parental support. Wrestling with these questions gives them opportunities to not only discover emergent meaning but also to learn how to cope with strong, powerful feelings.

Yet others, even with beautiful support from family, teachers, and friends, may need professional help. If your intuitive child is showing signs of depression or communicates concerns about feeling hopeless and meaningless about her life, I recommend seeking professional help. Depression is treatable and suicide is preventable. If you think your child is depressed, and especially if the child has mentioned any suicidal thoughts, it is vital to get help.

The Attention Deficit Disorder (ADD) Question

Attention deficit disorder (ADD) and attention-deficit/hyperactivity disorder (ADHD) are characterized by inattention, impulsivity, distractibility, and hyperactivity (in the case of ADHD).

ADD and occasionally ADHD share a couple of characteristics in common with some intuitive children; notably, distractibility and occasional spaciness. The two are quite different, however, as are their remedies. It is widely believed that the symptoms of ADD are caused by an imbalance of chemicals in the neurotransmitter fluids in the brain,[7] and because of this, treatment is targeted at rebalancing these levels, usually through psychotropic medications. The occasional spaciness and distractibility that comes with being highly intuitive and empathic, on the other hand, stems from dealing with things like multiple intuitive impressions arriving at once or trying to figure out where a sudden empathic pain is coming from.

The child might also be bored in the classroom or engaging in typical intuitive-style thinking, including pondering his own big-picture ideas and making intuitive leaps in thinking to the end of the lesson. When children can leap to the end result of a lesson (or even think they can), they sometimes find instructive details boring and tedious. Perhaps this boredom looks like ADD because the child isn't following the same linear, sequential learning steps as the majority of their classmates and is "off-point" on the given task. Thoughtful consideration of the child's intuitive learning style can often help sift through this distinction.

Critics of the ADD diagnosis often wonder if the child's ADD-like behaviors are simply a case of a poor fit between the learning environment and a child's style or needs. Along these lines, if you adjust the environment or challenge the child in ways that are a better fit, the behavioral characteristics of the ADD dissolve. Observing whether or not the symptoms disappear when the child is truly engaged in what she is doing could be one way of answering this question. If the child's behavior were simply due to a poor fit in the environment or boredom, it would appear that this could help separate out the boredom and poor fit issues from authentic neurotransmitter level problems. Because most classroom curricula do not take into account intuitive styles of learning, this issue can be accentuated for a highly intuitive child. Keep in mind, however, that not all highly intuitive children will have these issues.

After helping your child manage the stressors of having significant intuition and empathy, if you find that the child is still displaying significant ADD symptoms, you may want to consider a professional evaluation for treatment. If your child is responding with stress behaviors from being overwhelmed on the intuitive and empathic channels, a neurotransmitter drug designed to balance brain chemistry is probably not the answer. Rather, helping this child manage the influx of intuitive and empathic data could help the child to focus and be present. It is also possible that your child can be both highly intuitive and have a neurotransmitter imbalance, in which case solutions that take into consideration both sets of challenges may be appropriate.

Sensory Processing Disorder

Parents of very sensitive children, and particularly physically sensitive children, often witness their children struggling with heightened awareness of sensory input. Highly intuitive, empathic children are no exception to this phenomenon. Children may respond to these discomforts with requests to have tags pulled out of clothing and sock seams turned inside out, and they may have strong responses to foods. Interestingly, many of these behaviors are shared both by highly sensitive children, highly intuitive children, and those who struggle with sensory processing disorder (SPD).[8]

According to Carol Stock Kranowitz, author of *The Out-of-Sync Child: Recognizing and Coping with Sensory Processing Disorder,* "Sensory processing disorder is the inability to use information received through the senses in order to function smoothly in daily life...SPD happens in the central nervous system, at the 'head' of which is the brain. When processing is disorderly, the brain cannot do its most important job of organizing sensory messages."[9] In SPD, sensory information is abnormally processed through the nervous system, resulting in either hyposentivities or hypersensitivities. Hypersensitivities include discomforts with being touched (especially light touch), unexpected touch or being bumped into, eye contact discomfort, and pain from clothing tags and uncomfortable fabrics, to name a few. With hyposensitivity, the child experiences a lack of sensory input and actually seeks out more sensory stimulation. Kranowitz distills the SPD essence by pointing out, "The red flags are a child's unusual responses to touching and being touched or to moving and being moved."[10]

At first glance, it would appear that SPD and high intuition share little in common and are easily distinguishable on the basis of how the senses are impacted: SPD involves processing issues regarding the basic five senses and how they interface with the physical world, whereas intuitive empathy involves the sixth sense and how it is integrated via the other senses. But this distinction is not always so clear-cut. It would appear that some exceptionally intuitive, empathic children become so highly stimulated and upset by the volume of input they receive on these channels that their overload either results in or mimics sensory processing dysfunctions. If you have an intuitive child who is having trouble with sensory integration, help exists for your child. When a child is so deeply impacted by sensory discomfort that it negatively impacts their activities of daily living and learning, it is time to evaluate whether or not the child might be experiencing sensory integration problems. Traditionally, occupational therapists are the professionals to turn to for this kind of a problem. The child who is both highly intuitive and has sensory processing challenges could very well benefit from specific therapies for SPD.

Again, as with the ADD caution, SPD symptoms are certainly not experienced by all highly intuitive children. This connection is included to point out that if your child is experiencing sensory integration problems, you may want to investigate further so your child receives the right kind of support. Please bear in mind that if your child is experiencing sensory integration problems, he may be helped by the ideas presented in this book, but the specific needs of SPD are beyond the scope of this book.

Trauma and Intuitive Children

Children who are traumatized by living through an especially painful, shocking event are especially prone to feelings of hypervigilance, also known as the feeling of needing to be on guard all the time in order to stay safe. The keyed-up feeling of hypervigilance is very hard on the nervous system and can contribute to anxiety and exhaustion. I recommend professional therapy for traumatized children so they can heal from the trauma as soon after the traumatic event as is possible.

In some cases, a traumatic event may even accelerate or heighten a child's intuition. When a trauma goes unresolved, a child might automatically start to do more scanning of her environment to help predict and control other impending dangers. One of the ways the child might scan the environment is through a heightened use of intuition. The response of kicking intuition into overdrive is essentially an example of fanning out the "radar" to be able to scan people and the environment for future impending danger. In psychological terms, this is similar to hypervigilance, only with a twist. I view this use of hypervigilant intuition as an example of a child working too hard with her gift, but it is not necessarily a negative consequence. I've encountered many individuals over the years who credit their awakening of intuition to a particularly difficult or even traumatic event in their youth. For many of them, the acceleration of their intuition was later seen as a gift that offered a sense of solace and access to a dimension of awareness that was not as present prior to the difficult life event.

Finding Help for Your Child

If your child is experiencing anxiety, depression, or another mental-health challenge, I recommend that you seek out the help of a qualified professional who specializes in helping children with that problem. When you are interviewing a therapist, it will help if you can find one who is open to hearing about your child's intuitive experiences without pathologizing your child. The field of psychology is still evolving in its attitudes toward intuition, and you might encounter this bias within the profession as you speak with practitioners. A great child therapist need not share this trait, but I personally feel it is important that the therapist sees and respects children for who they are and not fault them for their intuitive lens on life. As you look for a therapist, remember to ask the questions you feel you need answered and use your own instinct in making a decision. I always encourage children to have a voice in the decision as well, by checking to make sure that the child feels comfortable with the therapist.

the care and keeping of intuitive, empathic bodies

My beliefs I test on my body,
on my intuitional consciousness,
and when I get a response there,
then I accept.

D. H. LAWRENCE

Intuitive children flourish when their bodies and boundaries are respected and they feel safe. Neglect these precious foundations and the child may be in for some discomfort. This chapter will look at why intuitives can experience unique body needs based on their sensitivities and what you can do to support your child in the areas of diet, sleep, and exercise or activity. You'll also learn about things that you can do to help your child feel more comfortable when she absorbs too much negativity.

If you are a parent lucky enough to have a strong constitution and rarely get sick or feel the pain of others, it might be hard to imagine that your child could be upset by the environment in a way that impacts his biology. Parents who do not share their child's unique characteristics might mistakenly interpret their child's sensitivities as weak, disingenuous, dramatic, overly sensitive, manipulative, imagined, or a cry for attention. If your child has an exquisitely sensitive system, which many intuitive children do, you may also become weary from working so hard to meet the physical and emotional needs of your child.

Intuitive children aren't trying to be irritating to their parents when they have odd and unique body needs. As mentioned in the stress chapter, the subtle neurobiology differences of these children simply give them *more* to deal with on a daily basis. We can't leave the body out of the equation because it is the instrument for collecting and registering the empathic data. Intuitive feelers experience so much through their bodies, especially when they are using their finely tuned capacities for somatic empathy.

The Body Doesn't Lie

We can fool our minds, but it is harder to fool the body. Remember Anna, the girl who had the gut-feeling intuition about the fugitive? A big part of Anna's intuition came in through her body signals that she registered as a warning. Body wisdom arrives in much the same way as an intuitive hunch. It bypasses the linear, rational mind to provide a lightning fast answer on the feeling channel. The child might know danger by the hair standing up on the back of her neck or by suddenly feeling sick and weak. Headaches, nausea, racing heartbeats, fear, and depression from out of the blue can all be possible signals of the arrival of intuitive data. The truth is that our bodies are all unique and our signals will vary. You and your child will come to know when something doesn't feel right. It is important to listen to these signals and, if needed, to act on them. As parents listen to and value their children's body signals, it helps the children to trust their own bodies and their own navigation systems.

Listening to the body is also *the* essential ingredient to teaching children how they can access their body's clues to help them know not only how to steer clear of danger, but also how to decide between an intuitive yes or no in making decisions. As you'll see throughout this book, intuitive children can routinely benefit from developing skills that help them tune out excess outside influence and tune in to their own sense of what's right for them and thus stay grounded in their own truth.

Teaching Children How to Trust
Their Inner Yes and No

When we are in a potentially dangerous situation and our intuitive bells and whistles are going off, we often don't have the luxury of weighing all the pros and cons. It can be helpful to have a crisp sense of inner-knowing so that we can seamlessly follow up with action if that is called for. In these situations, it is incredibly helpful to have already done the groundwork of building up confidence in trusting intuitive hunches. One of the ways that your child can build this confidence is to clearly know the difference between what a yes and no feels like in the body.

Our intuition can help to keep us safe, but it is not just designed to give us negative feedback. Part of the real fun of partnering with the body comes in feeling when your intuition is leading you to a yes in life. The yes responses have their own distinguishing body feelings that vary for all of us. Some of the many ways I have heard positive intuitive hunches described are: "It feels lighter all of a sudden," or feeling "happy in one's heart," "sparkly," "open," "expanded," "tickly," "a movement forward," "a vibration," "lit up," and so on. By contrast, I've heard a no described as feeling "sad," "off," "like jello," "flat," "dim," "darkened," "tight," and even "blank—just a nothing."

I have a fairly consistent way of tuning in to yes and no in my own body. A no feels like my throat is constricting, and a yes feels like a pleasant tingling sensation in the bottoms of my feet. The two sensations are distinct and have happened countless times over the years, helping me to shed light on decision making and bolster my confidence in my inner guidance. Of course, this learning process was gradual, and it took some time for me to recognize the connection between these specific areas in my body and intuitive guidance. The process is not foolproof, but time has shown it is a form of information I can confidently consider, along with what logic has to say.

One way to develop the ability to differentiate between an intuitive yes and no is to ask your body to show you a yes and wait to notice what that feels like in your body. It might feel like you are merely making up a yes, but just stay loose and nonjudgmental while the sensations arise. Then, ask your body to show you a no. Notice the differences in the sensations. Be patient with yourself and your child if this takes a few tries. The more you tune in to your body, the faster this will develop as a means of uncovering intuitive wisdom. A developing child may also discover that her own personal way of tuning in to yes, no, truth, danger, and other intuitive body signals changes over time. The deeper principle that is being anchored for intuitive children is that they can listen to and trust the intuitive language of their bodies.

Similarities to the Highly Sensitive Child

As we build our understanding of who the intuitive child is, it is helpful to take a look at the vanguard work of Elaine Aron, PhD, mentioned in the previous chapter, whose book series, starting with *The Highly Sensitive Person*, teaches that highly sensitive people have unique needs that must be met in order to thrive in the world. Intuitive children often have exquisitely sensitive systems and share many of the characteristics that Dr. Aron identifies in the trait of high sensitivity. As parents and adults meet the needs of their highly intuitive child, they frequently find they are helping the child learn how to live with unique body and temperament needs as well. The overlap traits for these two kinds of children will vary from child to child, but I find overlap with at least the following characteristics: difficulty getting to sleep after an exciting day, noticing the distress of others, being very sensitive to pain, being bothered by noisy places, noticing subtleties, feeling things deeply, and being intuitive.[1] If you have a child who has demonstrated sensitivity since birth, I recommend reading *The Highly Sensitive Child* by Dr. Aron for a wonderfully positive understanding of this trait.

When we realize that there is nothing wrong with having a sensitive body, we can get busy with the real work of learning how to protect it, nourish it, and give it what it needs to stay balanced. I know—as an intuitive adult with a highly sensitive body—that attentiveness makes a big difference in staying happy and balanced.

What We Can Learn from Holistic Therapies

Psychology is not the only profession to take notice of sensitive body types. In the course of my research, I was fortunate to have the input of Holly Guzman, LAc, OMD, a talented and experienced acupuncturist and Oriental Medicine Doctor, who helped shed light on the causes of hypersensitivity in the highly intuitive/empathic body.[2] She explained that in Chinese medicine the heart and small intestine share a relationship with one another and have an overlap of purpose in their function of absorbing nutrients and eliminating what is not useful. Food does not enter our body in a completely pure, useable form. Hence, the small intestine must be able to decide what to keep and what to release as waste. If it absorbs too little, we can be malnourished. If it lets too much in, as in leaky gut syndrome, it can be toxic.

In a somewhat parallel process, the heart has to be able to respond to human relationships and all of their imperfections. Human love rarely comes in a consistently pure form. As such, we have to know when not to absorb that which is better released as waste. This includes not absorbing other people's negativity, anger, shame, and other dense and even destructive emotions. Like the small intestine in its healthy state, the heart has its own innate wisdom of what is nourishing and smart to absorb and what is toxic and should stay outside the heart.

In Dr. Guzman's medical experience, she has witnessed many sensitive children struggling with the issue of being too open and absorbing too much into their systems. By contrast, she also encounters people whose bodies lack sensitivity and can't absorb enough of what they need. One of the tricks to attaining balance, therefore, is getting the right absorption/elimination ratio as a flow in the body. Our exquisite bodies are hardwired down to the cellular matrix for knowing when to say yes and no and keeping us in top shape. But we need some help now and then to strike the right balance. If you have a child who is experiencing difficulties on the physical level with maintaining balance, it might be helpful to find an alternative health practitioner who can support your child's health. Alternative practitioners who look at physical health at the energetic level include acupuncturists (many don't use acupuncture needles with children), homeopaths, naturopaths, chiropractors, and other professionals.

I am especially intrigued with the concept of balancing absorption and elimination rates when it comes to intuitive children. Most of the ten skills I recommend for intuitive children involve helping them to regulate their absorption of what they pick up from the environment, from people, places, and the world, and then eliminate or move out the energies that need to be released.

When it comes to raising intuitive, empathic children, their needs can often fall outside the basic areas that most parents would expect to deal with—and body needs are no exception. In the following section, we'll look at three key areas that can help to strike a balance in the physical lives of intuitive children: diet, exercise, and sleep.

Diet

All children should have a healthy diet, but when highly intuitive children don't eat right, it can throw off their intuitive and emotional system. Do you have a child who is a picky eater? How about one who is very clear about what foods make him feel better than others? What about a child who is sensitive to additives or food dyes? All of these characteristics can be symptomatic of a child who is physically sensitive, which is a characteristic of many highly intuitive children as well. Although these characteristics might create more work for a parent, perhaps they also serve a healthy function when it comes to a sensitive, intuitive child. For a child who thrives on the high-quality fuel of a nutrient rich, balanced diet, it can be very helpful to discern the foods that make the child feel lousy as well. When children cultivate the ability to know what foods make them feel good or bad, they might even be able to say no to the foods that make their taste buds happy momentarily but leave them feeling sick and off balance for much longer.

✳ John — age 5

Learning to Respect His Intuitive Guidance with Food

John was an example of a highly sensitive body. As an intuitive child who developed the skills to listen to his body and his hunger signals, John loved all the treats in life, but he also had some food allergies and declared himself a vegetarian at the age of 4 because he couldn't stand the thought of animals being killed for his food source. John could even tell if a food was organic or not based on the taste and how it felt to his body. He had the advantage of his family being able to buy fresh, organic produce from a local farm. On the occasions that John's mom fed him nonorganic produce, he'd ask her, "Is this organic?" but when it was organic, he wouldn't ask. Did John just have a highly discerning palate, or was he aware of his food on a more subtle level? Who knows? But it is clear that John was developing the ability to know what felt good inside of his body. He was also harnessing one of those assets of having a sensitive body that can "tune in" to what feels right to eat and take inside. I think that all of the effort that we put into feeding our children nutritiously and encouraging them to tune in to what their body hungers for can pay off in the long run by children learning how to do this for themselves when they are away from home—and certainly when they leave home.

Knowing how to check in with our bodies and respond to what we deeply hunger for is an essential skill for sensitive body types. As you help your child understand and listen to these needs, it might be helpful to consider the following questions: Do you know what kind of fuel your child runs best on? Do you notice mood differences related to any specific foods that your child eats? Is your child cultivating a positive relationship with food? Can your child read her own hunger signals and speak up for what she needs? Is your child starting to see the connection between how she feels emotionally with what she eats and drinks?

emotional responses to eating

Two areas that you may want to keep an eye on with your child are overeating and undereating in response to being emotionally and intuitively overwhelmed. Eating can be a source of comfort as well as nutrition. Children who discover that they feel better or can reduce the intensity of life through eating food can be at risk on the overeating end of the spectrum. For this type of child, you might want to pay attention to what the child is truly hungering for and notice if he eats for comfort. If this is the case, helping your child to state his emotional needs and receive loving attention from a parent can be a powerful redirect.

At the other extreme are the intuitive kids who may be picking up on so many upsetting feelings throughout the day that they lose their appetite. Of course, actual medical reasons are always important to investigate when this is happening regularly, including checking for food allergies and sensitivities. When the origin is not medically based, these children could benefit from developing skills to clear out other people's feelings and get back to the rhythm of their own needs—like hunger.

the other things we hunger for

Food and drink aren't the only things we hunger for as human beings. The kinds of inputs that we receive in the form of other people's words, moods, and treatment of us, as well as the experiences we expose ourselves to, make a big difference in our lives, maybe more than we even realize. Judith Orloff, MD, is a gifted intuitive empath, board-certified psychiatrist, and author of *Positive Energy: 10 Prescriptions for Transforming Fatigue, Stress and Fear into Vibrance, Strength & Love.* In her book, Dr. Orloff explains that it is vital to cultivate positive energy within our own lives and reduce the things that rob us of our life-force energy as much as possible. I recommend this book as a powerful support for adult intuitives.

As parents we can keep a finger on the pulse of what kind of larger "diet" our children ingest. If your child is particularly sensitive to other people's pain, it is essential for the child to know the joys, too. Does the child have enough input of the beauty of nature or the lightheartedness of jokes and stories? Is the child regularly exposed to positive thinkers and people who make meaning out of their lives, or who can just make the child laugh? Does your child know that it is okay, and even healthy, to excuse oneself from experiences, people, shows, and situations that are negative, hurtful, and cause deep pain? This isn't to say that children should regularly excuse themselves from facing and resolving conflicts or from being compassionate with others who are in pain. But it is an invitation to see when a steady diet of too much pain and too much caring has turned into a burden and is sapping the child's energy. If the child is simply "taking on" the other person's pain and the pain is shutting down the child, it is time to practice some of the skills taught in this book or just to take a break from the negative input altogether.

Exercise

Exercise is a vital part of staying healthy, especially for children who take on more than the average share of other people's feelings. I've spoken before about the importance of intuitive children feeling happy in their bodies and at home on earth, and exercise is a terrific way to support a feeling of being connected and grounded through walking, running, dancing, or however else your child's feet touch the earth.

Thankfully, most children don't think about the necessity of working out and exercising. Moving their limber bodies is fun and energizing and not a chore on the to-do list as it is for so many busy adults. When children are engaged in exercise, they are using their basic senses and learning about what they are physically capable of doing. All of the ways of moving the body through exercise are fantastically efficient ways of helping your intuitive child be grounded, without ever even having to discuss the concept of grounding.

However, not every child is as automatically inclined to get outside and exercise. It is so easy today for children to choose the television, a video game, or some other form of electronic entertainment that keeps them from what used to be the true childhood pastime of going outside to play and blow off steam. America's epidemic of sedentary children speaks to the need to remain mindful of a child's exercise levels.

Exercise is a great way of shaking off the energy the child has picked up from other people and situations during the day, and experiencing more of their own sense of self. Over the years I have also noticed something important in the lives of adult intuitives when they increase their exercise level: They feel stronger, more solid, more present, and more grounded. Sometimes a sensitive body can somehow leave us feeling at a disadvantage, and taking time to exercise on a regular basis and actually feeling the strength of one's body can have a positive carryover effect psychologically.

Sleep

Sleep is a delicious built-in recharger that can sometimes be disrupted for the intuitive child. If a child hasn't had sufficient opportunity to let go of the stimulus and energy of the day, this can manifest itself in trouble falling and staying asleep. Additionally, I have heard from numerous parents of intuitive children that their natural openness to intuitive information doesn't turn off when the lights go off at night. Sometimes this trait translates into insomnia, nightmares, night terrors, and a poor state of deep rest.

Intuitive children often possess very creative imaginations, which can ramp up at bedtime. The child may experience more than the average share of finding meaning in the things that go bump in the night. One of the reasons is that their minds are accustomed to jumping to intuitive conclusions. Children will often talk about their fears of monsters, boogeymen, and even intruders. It is developmentally normal for all children to go through this phase and learn to master their fear of the dark and of dangers that may lie in the unknowns of night. The intuitive child faces additional challenges in this area. Often, intuitive impressions and feelings will surface when outside activity has settled down and the child is lying still in bed. The child may also have a tougher time settling down due to the heightened sensitivity from the day and the state of arousal in the nervous system. If the child had a particularly active or upsetting day, with high levels of stress regardless of the source, it can be quite challenging for this child to settle down easily for sleep.

I find that many traditional ideas for getting children to sleep can be useful to a degree with intuitive children, but there are other needs usually not covered in most parenting books. The problem with intuitive children who can't get to sleep usually isn't that they aren't tired. The problem often is that they are experiencing intuitive and empathic overload.

One way this overload can manifest itself is in the form of unexpressed emotions pent up from the day. Some children hold on to these emotions and stressors throughout the day, only to realize when their head hits the pillow that they have something to tell you. The child might not be stalling for more time awake. If you have a child who routinely holds on to the stories of the day for the last few minutes before bedtime, as many highly intuitive children do, you might encourage your child to have some emotional process time about an hour before bed—or even earlier if possible. Another alternative, when parents decide that the emotional unloading is becoming too much of a hindrance to the bedtime routine, is to encourage older children to write down their worries in a notebook to review alone or with you the next day.

Falling asleep can mean so much more than just closing our eyes when our head hits the pillow. It is an invitation to let go of the day. Our bodies and psyches can be especially sensitive in this transition point of surrendering to sleep. One of the qualities that intuitive children often respond to at bedtime is the feeling of safety. If the feeling in their bedroom or house feels off to them, or unsafe in some way, it can disrupt the ease with which they can go to sleep. I find that it makes sense to pay attention to helping the child feel as safe as possible at bedtime so it becomes easier to let go into the unknown realm of darkness and sleep.

Home Energy Hygiene

Children who are antsy and unsettled at bedtime might be giving their parents clues about how their environment is feeling to them. Clues might come in the form of an agitated body that just can't seem to settle down to rest or comments like, "Something doesn't feel right in the house tonight" or "I just don't feel good in here tonight." When children drop clues about not feeling safe, it is an opportunity to help them feel safer by talking it out with them or taking some kind of action to reassure them. Maybe it is something as simple as the child picking up on an unresolved conflict that happened in the house during the day, or maybe the cause is somewhat more mysterious and complex as is illustrated in the following story.

✳ Josh — age 4

Not Feeling Safe in His Bedroom

Josh was 3 years old when his parents moved into a new home that came with a heap of baggage and sad stories. The previous owner had died in the house, and his family had a history of violent communication. Although there was a felt sense of sadness in the house, Josh's family thought that once they moved in and made it their own they would be able to turn it around and create a happy space. Neither parent could have predicted how hard it would be for Josh to sleep in this house. Highly sensitive, intuitive Josh struggled with the energy of the home. One night he came out of his bedroom saying, "Mom, there is an old man in my room and he is mean and smelly." Josh's mother ran to her child's room to find no such man, and she chalked up his experience to an active imagination. But the same thing happened night after night. Finally, exasperated with his insistence, she decided that she would treat the situation as if it were real. Sitting down on the side of the his bed, she demanded out loud, "This is Josh's room and you need to leave, sir! We live here now. We mean you no harm. We claim this space for Josh and our family." A little smile crept over Josh's face and he whispered to his mom, "He left." Josh never reported being bothered in this way again.

Josh's mom was willing to enter into her child's experience and help him feel safe. You can do the same whether your child is picking up on something intuitively or through his imagination. Whether it is an imagined monster in the closet or the feeling left over from the last tenant in the house, it is possible to help children feel safer by listening to them and participating in some meaningful way in order to reestablish their sense of safety.

The first step in this repatterning for safety is to listen to children and not judge the content of what they are expressing. Since it can be challenging to discern whether a child is dealing with an imagined or real intuitive disturbance, I like to take the stance of honoring the child's concerns no matter what. This helps children to feel heard and reassured by a protective adult who is joining with them in creating safety and a sense of sanctuary in the problem space.

It is especially important to feel safe in our bedrooms because this is the place where we completely surrender to sleep and let down our defenses. If the child doesn't feel safe environmentally, then it will impede the natural process of letting go and allowing for sleep. The good news is that you don't have to call in the Ghostbusters or be a psychic to clear the bad feelings in your home and help your child to feel safe. While it is serious business when a child can't fall asleep and a family is becoming increasingly sleep deprived, the means to clearing the space don't have to be so serious. The following ideas for space clearing come from both spiritual and secular sources. I encourage you to use the suggestions that have meaning for your family and be creative with making up your own with the help of your child. Experiment and find out which of the following works for you and your child:

★ In the Native American tradition, sage is dried and made into a bundle called *smudge*. The bundle is lit, and the smoke is used during ceremonies and for personal use specifically to purify and expel bad energy both inside and around a person. Smudge sticks are readily available today and can be easily used for the intention of clearing the home.

★ If you have a drum or musical instruments in the house, you can beat the drum, clap, and make music in the space. Try creating original songs that express your intention for restoring the sacred space for your child's sleep.

★ Call upon protection (such as a child's guardian angel) or imagine a protective creature coming into the room to help clear away fear and keep the child safe.

★ Concentrate your prayerful intention with speaking out loud in the room, "This is [child's name] room and we intend for this to be a clear, loving space where he [or she] can play and have sweet dreams throughout the night."

★ Create a protection shield for the child's bedroom that can hang above the child's bed. It is important that the child take the lead on the creation of the shield, although if the child would like your assistance and even your mark of protection above her bed, I think that is wonderfully symbolic.

Additional Settling at Bedtime

Because intuitive children can tend toward arousal in their nervous systems, it is helpful to look toward those bedtime interventions that help to settle and calm the nervous system as much as possible. A regular bedtime ritual can help give children a sense of structure and security as they let down any guards they may have been holding up from the day. A brief foot or back massage with a relaxing body oil can be a welcome sleep inducer, especially from loving hands that are expressing the intention of a peaceful sleep for the child. Chamomile tea, warm milk, and listening to relaxing music are all traditional tricks for helping the body to quiet itself for sleep. Some children might also benefit from the use of guided imagery before falling asleep to help the nervous system calm down. I've included a sample script and encourage you to be creative in designing a comforting guided imagery for your own child. Don't forget to ask your child for help in designing the imagery for sleep, because children often have terrific ideas about what works and what doesn't work.

guided imagery for falling asleep

Begin by having children get into bed. Gently tell them to close their eyes and begin breathing very slowly and deeply, using full breaths all the way in and all the way out. Periodically tell them that with each breath they are becoming more and more relaxed. Do this for about three minutes. Then begin the visualization, speaking in a quiet and calm voice.

Imagine you are inside a big, beautiful bubble. You are completely safe inside this bubble. No worries or any bad things can get in. Good things can come in if you want them to. Inside, the bubble is quiet and peaceful. You might hear some soft music, or maybe it is just quiet—whatever you want. There are wonderful scents inside the bubble as well (have your child choose the scents). (Pause). And now, you notice that inside the bubble you are lying on top of a big, fluffy, soft cloud. It is so soft and cozy, and you can feel how it cradles you. (Pause). And it begins to rise up in the air, gently rocking you back and forth. You float up through the ceiling without a sound, into the night sky. You are warm and protected in your bubble and on your cloud. The beautiful stars are twinkling above you as you gently float through the sky, and you feel calm and content. You snuggle your body into just the right position on your magic cloud, as your body grows calmer and calmer. All is well, and it is safe for you to let go now and go to sleep. You are safe and protected and all is well.

boundaries

A "no" uttered from deepest conviction
is better and greater that a "yes"
merely uttered to please,
or what is worse,
to avoid trouble.

MAHATMA GANDHI

Healthy boundaries are vitally important in human relationships. This chapter looks at the nuances of psychological, interpersonal, and energetic boundary setting in the life of an intuitive child. It is also the backdrop for learning skill number eight, distinguishing your energy from someone else's, which you'll learn more about in Chapter 8.

The same energy-sensing radar that intuitive children have for taking in good feelings and "knowing" things about people and places can also put them at risk for taking on negative energy. Are intuitive kids destined to be sponges to whatever the emotional climate is around them? No. But they may have to work a little harder to fortify their boundary-setting skills both psychologically and energetically.

Fortunately, we can learn boundaries like any other life skill. Did you ever have a moment when you were convinced your child wouldn't master some important skill? Riding a bike perhaps, or even potty training? With practice, we do learn our life skills, and setting boundaries is one of them. Good boundaries are important for helping an intuitive child feel comfortable and for keeping intuitive messages clear.

All children have the ability to learn to set healthy boundaries as a means to taking care of themselves physically and emotionally, the most basic boundary being the word "no." If a child has had an exhausting day and a friend calls up begging to play, being able to say, "Sorry, not today," respectfully and without giving into guilt is an important skill to have. Or if a bully at school is pestering a child, standing up for oneself or getting some help from an adult would be an act of self-care.

This, of course, is also true for the intuitive child. However, intuitive children need to learn more than just behavioral boundary skills. They also need to learn how to set boundaries with the unspoken, invisible information around them. In other words, instead of having their receiver tuned in to every single channel around them and experiencing chaotic static, they need to learn how to tune their receiver only to what is most important and tune out what isn't. This ability involves learning to prioritize intuitive impressions, which is an important skill that can take some time to develop. One of the most important steps in the prioritizing process involves the ability to distinguish between one's own thoughts and feelings, and the thoughts and feelings of others. You will learn more about how to support your child with this vital skill in Chapter 8, using skill number six (see page 131).

When children are particularly sensitive to the feelings of other people, they may need extra encouragement in utilizing their boundaries because they might not want to upset other people. You may want to remind your child that even though it might feel uncomfortable to stand up for oneself, doing so is an important part of life and friendships. When children see their parents modeling good boundaries at home, they also get a flavor for how this works and then can apply it in the world around them. So the next time you feel irritation for having to establish yet another parenting boundary with your child, remember that your effective modeling goes far in giving your child the permission to do the same in his life.

Ducks and Sponges: Why Some Children Need More Support in Learning How to Set Boundaries

To further illustrate why your intuitive, empathic child may need extra support in learning about and setting boundaries, the following ducks and sponges analogy is a reminder that all children don't experience the same degree of challenge with boundary setting. This analogy suggests that ducks have an easier time with this skill than the sponges.

For duck people, the emotions of others just seem to roll off them like water off a duck's back. This duck-type of individual isn't necessarily a bad communicator. To the contrary, they can be very effective communicators who don't need to take the extra steps outlined in this book. In fact, they can have their feet held to the fire in a major conflict and move on to their next activity unscathed. By contrast, intuitive empaths tend to be sponges, physically registering the feelings of others with whom they come into contact. An intuitive empath rarely walks away from a conflict without having a multitude of physical feelings and ruminations on the nature of the conflict.

Ducks and sponges often misunderstand each other. Ducks think that sponges are overly sensitive, high maintenance, and emotionally unbalanced. Sponges think that ducks are insensitive, lacking in empathy, and oddly quick to move on after upsetting situations.

If you have a child who can be a sponge to the emotions of others, you can probably see the value in helping your child to learn when he is doing so and how to comfort his state of arousal and calm down. Children don't decide to engage in this behavior; it almost always just happens automatically. Because it is an automatic body experience, it is easy to think, "This must be my feeling." But it might not be. These children have to learn to distinguish their feelings from those of others so they aren't plagued by mistakenly taking on their friends' stomachaches, headaches, and bad moods.

With practice, children get better and better at transforming their experience from one of sponge to a finely tuned body system that provides incredible insight into how other people may be feeling. In this way they learn that their empathic abilities can be their allies and that they can tap into this intuitive source, take what's useful, and then move on. When children don't learn how to move on after pulling in upsetting empathic data, it can be very tiring. Can you imagine the burden of bearing a whole classroom's worth of feelings? Talk about exhausting! The following story demonstrates how these skills are anchored in real-life teachable moments.

✳ Emma — age 8
Learns to Distinguish Her Sadness from a Friend's

It was Memorial Day and Emma woke up content after a great night's sleep. She ate a big breakfast and went on to play with a bunch of new toys and games that she'd been looking forward to enjoying on this holiday from school. Her mood was content. Unexpectedly, two hours into her carefree day had begun, she began to feel awful and depressed. Her mom offered her the usual methods for rebalancing—food, love, a change in activities—but nothing helped Emma to shift out of the dark emotions that had hit from out of the blue. About forty-five minutes later, her best friend Taylor called in tears. Her favorite pet hamster was missing and she wanted to talk it over with Emma. As Emma spoke empathically with Taylor on the phone that morning, her mom watched as Emma's own emotions started to lift. Incredibly, when Emma got off the phone her inexplicable sad mood had lifted. Emma never lost her ability to be present to her friend on the phone. She was beautifully empathetic as are so many intuitive empath children with their friends, but somehow learning about her friend's sad news had started to lift the inexplicable sadness off her.

About an hour later, Emma's mom deduced that Emma felt her unexpected dive in emotion about the same time that Taylor discovered her hamster was missing. Her mom decided to share her theory about this coincidence with Emma, who made the conscious connection and excitedly said, "Mom, that's it! That's why

I was sad but I didn't know it." They went on to talk about how it is possible sometimes to feel someone else's emotions. Emma's mom realized this teachable moment would help her daughter to discern between her own feelings and those of someone else. They specifically looked at how the feeling suddenly appeared and also at the fact that she had been feeling great just before it descended. Emma and her mom had the bonus of being able to hear the information (missing hamster, upset best friend) within hours of the emotional upset. With such quick feedback, both Emma and her mom were able to reflect on the details of what was happening in real time.

I think of these kinds of learning experiences as real gifts for intuitive children and their parents. We aren't always this lucky to receive specific feedback on why a mood suddenly descends. But when we have a teachable moment like this one, it generates information about what it feels like to be on the receiving end of someone else's distress. When it happens again, the child can experiment with pulling in his own intuitive antenna, as discussed in skill number two located in Chapter 8 (see page 121).

Emma's experience is a good example of stressful feelings originating from a purely intuitive place rather than an emotionally empathic place. We know this because Emma was not in close physical proximity to Taylor. Taylor lived ten minutes away, and they had no contact that day until Taylor called to say that her hamster was missing. In terms of teasing out the origin of Emma's distress in this situation, it feels to me as though this kind of discernment is much more advanced than dealing with empathic boundaries.

The Differences Between Intuitive and Empathic Boundaries

With empathic boundaries, you have the advantage of seeing another person's face and reading body language, so it is easier to determine the origin of the feelings. Intuitive boundaries, such as what Emma dealt with that day, are often trickier because they happen in a vacuum of not knowing where the upset is coming from—usually not until later. In my experience, these kinds of boundaries can take quite a long time to learn about for most people due to the absence of accessible data. Sometimes, the only practical thing to do in these murky situations is to ask, "Is this feeling mine, or does it belong to someone else?" or simply get busy with another activity that refocuses your attention. This refocusing is one way to pull in the intuitive antenna. You will learn more about this skill in Chapter 8.

Parents, teachers, and therapists can all benefit from realizing that when an intuitive child is having a meltdown, it is possibly due to the child taking on someone else's feelings—empathically and/or intuitively. This is a subtle emotional transaction that may fly under the radar of most adults. Many sensitive children will hold on to this kind of information in private, scared that other people would think it is crazy, or they may not even know what is happening. Holding on to upsetting feelings about others all by yourself, particularly when you are a child, can cause quite a bit of stress. One remedy is to ask the upset child to notice if he is feeling someone else's pain. If he is, then it is an opportunity for you to encourage him to make the decision to let it go. If you find that your child is experiencing difficulty in this area, you might want to also pay close attention to the sixth skill, teaching energy hygiene, located in Chapter 8.

The Importance of a Clear Yes or No in Boundary Setting

In Chapter 5, we looked at how to become aware of intuitive messages in the body in order to discern a yes from a no. This process is applicable to setting boundaries as well. The appropriate use of yes and no in our lives saves a lot of grief, and it goes far in protecting our precious energy systems when put into action. Take time to teach your intuitive child all the ways to tactfully say no when necessary, and especially how to say no with power and determination when needed for situations of safety.

One of the essential ingredients of boundaries is realizing that sometimes we don't know they've been violated until they are crossed. Anger is often a signal that a boundary infringement has occurred. When this signal registers for children, it indicates they may need to say something or take some kind of action. It can be an opportunity to practice conflict resolution skills. I will discuss this skill in greater detail in Chapter 7.

If your child is having trouble with bad dreams or other figures of the imagination, teach your child to say no to what frightens her in this realm. In addition, if your child feels that someone is "sending" her bad feelings (for example, anger) that are affecting her, your child can say no to taking in these feelings.

Sometimes when children have trouble standing up for themselves and saying no to others, it is an opportunity for growth. Sensitive intuitive children don't like to hurt other people's feelings, and setting boundaries might not come naturally. With their parents' help, they can master this important skill. The following are some points to keep in mind about boundaries:

★ Saying no to others is important in relationships.

★ Saying no, and truly meaning it, impacts how other people respond to boundaries.

★ Looking to other people to define personal boundaries is backward.

★ Learning how to survive other people's disappointments when we say no is an important lesson.

★ Paying attention to what you want will inform your boundary setting.

★ Feeling angry can naturally happen when boundaries are crossed.

★ Being assertive about your needs is something that can be learned.

★ Visualizing a protection bubble can help with challenging energetic boundaries.

★ Asking for help in mastering boundary setting is natural and healthy.

Visualizing a Protection Bubble

In addition to psychological and interpersonal boundaries, it is useful for intuitive children to learn some form of energetic boundaries.

Guided imagery can be effective in supporting children with their energetic boundaries. One of the visualizations I use frequently in my work with intuitives is the concept of the bubble for protection. The protection bubble is an example of harnessing the imagination to help strengthen energetic boundaries. The following is a visualization of the protection bubble that you can use for your child or for yourself. Go ahead and use your own intuition to adapt it to your child's needs.

> *Begin by taking a few deep breaths and imagine that your body and mind are safe and calm. It is peaceful here and you are connected to the earth and the earth loves that you are a part of life. Imagine that you have a bubble of light around you and there is lots of space for you. As you focus on the bubble, it becomes sparkly and filled with a beautiful color (choose the color) that makes you feel cozy and safe. Take a look at the edges of your bubble. Are there any holes in it or leaks? If you find anything that needs repairing, use your imagination to fill in those holes now. It is very safe to be in your own bubble, and loving and friendly feelings can come in and all the things you need protection from can stay on the outside of your bubble. Finish by decorating your bubble if you want. How about putting a warrior, warrioress, or protective animal outside your bubble for extra protection. Do you want this protection in front of you, in back, on your sides, or in every direction? You are in charge of the design, so go ahead and let your imagination tell you what it needs.*

If a child is having difficulty with a particular person or situation, at the end of the bubble exercise the parents can say they are going to help test the strength of the child's bubble by bringing in the image of the person, place, or thing that is the challenge. For example, a parent can say, "Now we are going to imagine that (name the person or thing) is here on the outside of your bubble and you get to just stay in the safety of your own space. This person can't hurt you anymore or take away your happiness." Have the child take a few deep breaths and come back with eyes open to share with the parent what the experience was like. If the child had trouble staying in the bubble when the feared object was brought to mind, the parent can continue the exercise by asking the child if there is anything else he needs to imagine in order to feel safe.

The bubble concept can be adapted to whatever a child is dealing with at the time and is limited only by imagination. Here are a few more ideas.

fixing the leaky bubble

Sometimes it can be helpful to have the child identify any weaknesses or holes in the bubble, and to identify which circumstances or people tend to weaken it. If the child is having trouble with putting up psychic boundaries, have the child imagine what it would feel like to be in a weak or leaky bubble and ask, "Does anyone try to pop your bubble with words or hurtful actions? Do other people's sadness, worries, or anger get past the edge of your bubble? Why does this happen? Would you like that to be different? Is there anyone in your life whom you find it hard to say no to or with whom your bubble goes weak? What would you like to do about this?" You can have your child imagine fixing the bubble and making it stronger, and then follow up by repeating the previous bubble visualization.

Put It in a Bubble

Expanding on the bubble theme, children can also be asked to imagine a separate bubble that can be used help take things away. Have the children put all their cares, worries, and things they want to let go of into the flyaway bubble and release it into the sky. You can tailor this exercise to your family's spiritual beliefs. For example, children can give their bubble of cares to an angel or to God so that they don't have to carry the burden by themselves.

Some children do not respond much to the bubble concept, and older children may even find it to be childish. You know your child best. Some children prefer to have a sense of going into the vastness of the universe instead of being limited by the concept of a bubble. In this case, I recommend a more expansive visualization, such as the following.

Close your eyes and take a few deep breaths. Start by seeing yourself connected to the center of the earth by a cord. Now imagine that you are sitting on a magic carpet that slowly begins to rise off the ground. It rises higher and higher into the air, out into the night sky. Below you, you can see your house, then your city, state, country, and then the entire earth as you fly into outer space, totally safe, warm, and comfortable.

Rebalancing after Boundary Intrusions

Learning how to practice healthy boundaries is a gradual learning experience. For those times when children miss boundary cues and end up taking in toxic emotions, they can learn to move these emotions out of their systems through some form of self-expression. Here are a few ideas to get you started:

⋆ Have the child visualize the thing that is bothering her. Then have the child imagine this situation shrinking smaller and smaller until it is so small you can just blow it away or brush it off like a piece of dust. If the discomfort returns, use this imagery as much as needed until it removes the emotional charge.

⋆ Is the feeling stubborn like a brick wall? Imagine removing bricks from the bottom or top of the wall until the whole wall collapses, removing the obstacle.

⋆ Experiment with any creative activity that your child feels guided to do until her heart feels clear again. You can finish off the process by having your child draw a picture of her heart after the clearing to see if all is clear or if there is still some work to be done.

★ Draw a picture in a circle that contains all of the negative feelings and then let the child crumple it up, rip it up, and throw it into the trash can.

★ Blow up a balloon and imagine it is filled with the upset feelings; let the child pop it or stomp on it.

★ Provide a lump of clay and let the child poke it, slam it, and put his feelings into the clay.

★ Don't forget to visualize your own heart in a clear space so that you can be a positive role model and reassure your child that you want him to share the whole range of his feelings with you. Hold the confidence that your child can and will work it through.

When Boundaries Become Complicated for Children

One complication involving children and safety is that they are often in situations throughout their lives where they can't simply walk away; for example, a conflict that arises during instruction with a teacher, coach, or other caregiver. How do they practice self-care and boundary setting when they are dependent for care from an adult who is emotionally off balance, overly controlling, or frequently angry? It can be quite tricky for the child. For the sensitive and perceptive intuitive child, the tendency can be toward healing the situation so it improves immediately. But this can be a slippery slope for children because they experience an unnatural sense of power in the adult world.

I think it is cleaner psychologically for children to know that they can be supported by us to remove them from harmful situations and additionally that they have tools to deal with surprise encounters of negativity. We can also teach our children to remember that they have a right to leave the bad energy on the outside of their energy bubble. If it catches them by surprise, they can imagine they are pulling up the shield of their protection as quickly as possible.

✳ Erin — age 6
Having Complicated Boundaries Regarding a Teacher

Erin's story involving a difficult substitute teacher is an example in complicated boundaries for an intuitive child. Erin rarely talks about the deeper emotional component of her day when school ends. When that bell rings, she darts for her mom and a quick hug, then it is on to the monkey bars where she hangs, twists, skips bars, and lets loose with her peers. But come the evening, Erin usually has more than a few emotionally challenging situations to replay in her mind and maybe even talk about. One day Erin's troubles came tumbling out right after school when she had a substitute teacher who in her words was "the worst teacher ever of her whole life." She went on to recount how the teacher criticized, belittled, and disrespected the children. She was incredulous that the teacher was even allowed in the classroom for the day. Filled with the pain that she had witnessed during the day, she said, "Mom, I felt like I just wanted to cry…and some of the kids did."

Unfortunate? Yes. Irreparable? No. The first line of response was to listen fully to her whole story while giving her lots of permission for expressing all of her feelings. After an afternoon of being together and lots of holding hands and comforting, she later asked her mom, "If I made a very big mistake, something like breaking your wedding ring—would you still love me? What would you do? Would you get mad?" Erin's mom reassured her that yes, it is natural to make mistakes and yes she would always be there for her, loving her. Mistakes don't make love go away. We learn from them and we can fix the broken thing. From that chat with her mom, Erin was able to internalize the message that she could safely be herself, even if she made a very big mistake.

When children witness cruelty in the classroom or outside in the world, it is natural for them to try to make sense of it. For intuitive children, a cruelty to a friend is a vicarious cruelty to them. When intuitive children watch the cruelty happen, they take it in through all their sensory channels and it can become lodged in their bodies. Not only do they see and hear it, they can also feel empathetically what it is like for the other child to be shamed, blamed, and taunted. As parents, we can help dislodge the negativity first of all by helping children to sort out what it is they are feeling and helping them notice if the pain is personal or belongs to someone else. This can get a little tricky because the intuitive child feels so deeply for the injustice of others that it can feel as though it truly *is* his own grievance. But the task of processing through the feelings the child vicariously absorbed and shifting the negativity remains. You can help your child via art, reassuring words, hugs, and by reminding him that it is not his job to hold the anger or disappointment of someone else in his body.

When a Situation Is Beyond Energy Deflection Skills

Is your child in a situation in which a teacher or caregiver is using shaming, blaming, or questionable and manipulative behavior-management techniques? When a child is in a situation where this is occurring, it requires a solution bigger than the energy deflection skills outlined in this book. I think that young children especially need our fullest protection from such potentially damaging interactions. Questions you can ask yourself are, "Is this situation potentially damaging to my child's self-esteem or spirit?" and "Does my child come back to balance shortly after a debriefing of what happened and some rebalancing skills to remove the feelings of others that have been absorbed?" What does your own intuition say about the situation?

Empowered Boundaries and Exercising Flexibility

As an adult, are you comfortable with setting boundaries? Most parents (if not all!) have had to deal with plenty of boundary setting around issues such as giving into whining kids, setting time limits around activities, and limiting television time. Sometimes a parent has to say no to wonderful friends and activities because her child is simply maxed out for the day and needs a break. When we have to cancel a commitment because a child is overwhelmed, it can be awkward, uncomfortable, and even disappointing. If your intuitive child is also highly sensitive, you are probably no stranger to the territory of setting your own limits to accommodate your child's unique needs.

One of the best ways to teach your child the good graces of boundary setting is to practice it in your own life. Our children learn by example and are watching our successes and failures. So go ahead and enjoy your own freedom to use yes and no wisely in your life.

It is important to set and maintain your own boundaries in parenting because it will also help your child feel safe. If a child doesn't know where the limits are in the family and in the parenting relationship, it can make a child feel confused and insecure. Part of the reason for this is that it gives the child premature power. For example, when children never hear "No" because their parents are afraid of disappointing them or being seen as mean, children hear a message that they can usually get their way. Clear limits and expectations also give children something to push up against psychologically as they mature. Intuitive children need boundaries and limits just like other children. In fact, in some indigenous practices around the world, intuitive children are parented with some unique boundary-setting methods that teach them about the socially appropriate use of their extrasensory abilities. You'll learn more about about the use of these techniques in Chapter 10 on indigenous wisdom.

Intuitive Needs vs. Childhood Wants: Savvy Boundaries

Listening for the difference in intuitive needs versus childhood wants can be important in parenting, because children can be communicating a truth about what they truly need, which might be missed through the lens of traditional parenting that assumes parents always know best. If a child is badgering a parent for an ice cream cone, we can assume this is a childhood want. It obviously wouldn't be right to give in to every request for an ice cream cone. On the other hand, if the child tuned in to the need for a visit to a particular place in nature or to learn a particular skill, such as meditation even at an early age, a parent's ear might hear the uniqueness of that request. If that spirit request makes you feel like your child is on to something important—listen to it. This can be your child's inner direction coming through.

Journaling Questions about Boundaries

If this chapter touches something in you about the need to fortify your own boundaries, you may find the following journaling questions helpful in your exploration. The questions are also designed for further reflection in supporting your intuitive child in this skill area.

* ⋆ *Do you feel that setting boundaries is mean?*

* ⋆ *Was it acceptable to say no and have your preference heard and respected in your home as a child?*

* ⋆ *What does it feel like to set a boundary with your spouse, children, coworkers, strangers, and family of origin?*

* ⋆ *If you practiced more intentionality around the appropriate use of the word no, would there be more room for an enthusiastic yes for what positively lights up your life?*

* ⋆ *How are you modeling healthy boundary setting for your child?*

* ⋆ *Do you give equal messages of permission for boundary setting to your male and female children?*

* ⋆ *What is your vision of healthy boundaries for your child?*

* ⋆ *In what ways is your intuitive child struggling with or thriving with boundary setting?*

* ⋆ *Does your child have time to safely chill out and take a break from exercising boundary setting, or just let his intuition roam*

free if the child so chooses? Is there one area that you would like to focus on to help your child?

★ *What happens when your child is around someone who is very negative or in an environment that feels toxic? Can the child make the connection with how it makes her feel? Does your child know she can speak with you about these impressions and trust that you both can work toward solutions?*

parenting
the intuitive child

There is no instinct like that of the heart.

LORD BYRON

Parenting an intuitive child is like taking an extra-credit course in parenting that involves advanced material. For some parents, this class might seem like it is being conducted in a foreign language. Because your child is living with this extra helping of intuition and empathy, it impacts all aspects of life. The impact can be especially felt at home in the parenting relationship where communication takes a different shape than the norm. In this chapter, you'll learn about how to skillfully adapt your communication to meet the unique needs of your child. We'll look at why it is so important to come from a place of respect and authenticity, what builds emotional trust, and what happens when you, as a parent, don't honor your child's perceptions. We'll also explore how your child might be impacting your marriage and the importance of not only clear communication but great conflict-resolution skills as well.

Intuitive children are keenly aware of how adults deliver information to them. Because the modeling we give them is so valuable and they are looking to us to be their emotionally steady person, I think it is useful to spend some time in support of *you* as the parent in the trenches. Therefore, the second half of this chapter offers tips and techniques for taking care of yourself.

Your Intuitive Child Is Watching You Closely

Intuitive children are incredibly sensitive to the feelings of the most important people in their lives: their parents and adult caregivers. I have watched these children spot the slightest muscular movement on an adult's face and read it with the utmost accuracy. What is astonishing for most parents, however, is when their child is able to read their emotional state even when the parent is silent and hidden from view. The empathy can be so great that it quietly falls over into the land of mind/emotion reading. This can become a real problem for parental privacy.

No parent is perfect, and it is completely human to have those days of experiencing deep frustration. With intuitive children it might not be enough to zip your lips when you're losing your cool. If they so much as feel the emotion, it can still hurt. So what is a well-meaning parent of an intuitive child to do? Behavioral perfection is not possible, nor does it serve as a good role model. Part of the challenge is to do our best in being honest with ourselves and communicating with integrity. If there is a conflict that needs to be resolved, try to work it out. If your emotional state is affecting your child, experiment with ways of protecting them from feeling burdened by what you're feeling.

The Importance of Congruency in Communicating with Your Child

One of the unique traits of intuitive children is their extreme sensitivity to incongruities; they want our words, body language, and the emotional vibration to match up (also known as emotional congruency). If the emotion and the words don't match up, they sense the mismatch. For example, it is confusing to children to hear praise when they pick up on a frustrated, impatient, or insincere feeling behind it. Of course, intuition can get its signals crossed and a child can be seeing something that isn't there in another person, which is why it is important that we teach children to check out their intuitive hunches about people and situations. It is healthy to name the feeling we are having or the problem we are experiencing with those to whom we are close.

When your child picks up on some emotional distress you're experiencing and asks what's wrong and you say, "nothing," when it is actually a big "something," the child becomes confused and worried. If intuitive children repeatedly experience this reaction, they begin to mistrust their feelings and their sense that something is off. It can leave them feeling disconnected in the family, as it gives them the message that it is okay to be emotionally dishonest. When intuitive children pick up on an emotional distress signal from parents, they often personalize it and worry that it is something about them or something that they should fix.

Assuming that your emotional distress isn't about them, an alternative response to the "What's wrong, Mom? Are you upset with me?" question could be something like this: "I'm feeling tired and frustrated with something, but it's not about you." You could also add, "I think it would help me if I could take a few minutes of quiet." A statement like this doesn't give the child too much information. It clarifies that your upset is not caused by or directed at your child and underscores that you know how to take care of yourself. A response like this one gives space for a parent's privacy and lets the child know that the mood that they are sensing in the parent has nothing to do with them and requires no action on their part. The child can let it go.

Being emotionally congruent doesn't mean that parents share every little detail of experience with their children. Boundaries are absolutely essential in parenting, and parental privacy is healthy. When we speak and act from a commitment to be congruent, we have options. When we are congruent in our communication, we also contribute to emotional safety because children learn they can trust our words. They aren't put into the position of needing to guess the hidden message behind words that don't seem to match the feelings they are receiving.

When we communicate with honesty that is respectful, as in this last example, it invites the child to reconnect when stressful feelings are interfering with the connection. When we believe that children can rise to this skill level, it honors their abilities as communicators and gives them power to make a difference in relationships. They also learn that they can trust their feelings and can tell when they're out of connection with someone they love and depend on, and this can reassure them that they can do something about getting back to a safe place inside. This practice builds security and confidence in relationships, and is an important skill they will have for life.

How Intuitive Children Can Tune in to Your Marriage

One of the big surprises to parents of intuitive children can be their ability to tune in to the unspoken feelings in relationships—including the parenting relationship. Angela was mad at her husband for something, but she didn't want to discuss it at the time. She went about her day and by that evening when her 2-year-old daughter, who knew nothing of the conflict, saw her dad, she said, "Mean Daddy, I want Mommy!" She refused to hug him or hang out with him that evening until Angela had made peace with her husband. Talk about emotional transparency. Angela was shocked when she realized that her little girl was capable of naming her unspoken feelings out loud. She understood that her daughter's intuition posed a challenge that would force her to develop clearer communication with her husband. This translated into clearing unexpressed, conflicted emotions with her husband so that her daughter wouldn't be the one to speak for her. It was frustrating sometimes to feel like she was being held to a higher standard in parenting than other parents whose children were impervious to their subtle frustrations. Her daughter's innocent acting out of her mom's emotions, however, proved to be a reminder that it was worth the extra effort of keeping their communications as up-to-date and connected as possible.

As a marriage and family therapist, I can tell you that *all* children benefit when the emotional feeling in the family is clear and harmonious. Creating a feeling like this isn't magical; it comes from clear communication, loving kindness, and living with a clear intention to stay connected to one another. As parents we are able to set that tone in our families and model honest, intimate communication. This role modeling starts with how our children experience our adult relationships—not only the words that come out of our mouths, but also the feelings behind them.

The Pros and Cons of Being a Sensate Parent to an Intuitive Child

In Chapter 1, I explained that most parents possess a sensate system of perceiving the world as opposed to the intuitive system according to the Myers-Briggs typologies. Parents who have a dominant sensate lens on life, with less of an intuitive function, can feel perplexed at times by raising a highly intuitive child. The ways that you and your child experience the inner life and the outer world might leave you struggling for common ground and scratching your head as you try to figure out your child's motivations, sensitivities, and needs. Know that you aren't alone. Many sensate parents find themselves parenting highly intuitive children.

Parents who do not share the gift of heightened intuition and empathy can still be every bit as effective as parents who do. These parents can have a keen clarity about what is needed out in the world for the child to survive and are comfortable pushing a bit and holding steady with the view of a practical, grounded movement toward maturity. Sensate parents can act as a bridge of confidence for the intuitive child to the world at large. Successful parenting of an intuitive child by sensate parents can help the child feel grounded and comfortable in the world. Ideally, well-attuned parenting by a sensate parent helps the intuitive child learn how to blend the gifts of the intuitive realms with the practical know-how that a child will need before launching out into the world.

On the other hand, if the child's temperament and gifts have been misunderstood and marginalized, the child can feel that his true self is not being seen and accepted. If you are an extremely practical, I-believe-it-if-I-can-see-it kind of person and you're having trouble understanding your intuitive child, there is hope. You can practice connecting with your child without judging his distinctly different lens on life. The fact that you are reading this book speaks to your desire to understand your child's unique attributes and needs. Additionally, your child can benefit greatly from having a friendship with a trusted adult or older friend who shares the child's approach to life.

Children and Conflicts

Conflicts are a part of life. Most intuitive kids prefer to avoid them. It is uncomfortable to be exposed to them. Children who are empathic at the intuitive/kinesthetic level feel an outer conflict in their bodies. Ouch, no wonder your child wants to avoid the pain. Conflict is uncomfortable for them because they are wired for feeling everything through their bodies, including the denser and stronger emotions of others. It can be very empowering for intuitive children to see they can do something with the strong feelings that they register in their bodies, including learning when a tension has to do with them and working it out or letting go of conflicts that are not their responsibility.

It is unrealistic to shelter these children from every conflict, no matter how big or small. But you can have some guidelines when it comes to working through conflicts. I am passionate about people learning effective conflict resolution skills. When we have the conflict resolution skill set and use it, we anchor the understanding that conflicts are not something to be feared. When we find our way to the other side of a conflict and back to emotional safety, it can actually deepen a relationship. I think this is great modeling for children and something that will serve them in all of their relationships. Without it, intuitive children might be at risk for not being assertive about their needs in relationships, saying yes when they actually mean no, and not feeling the safety and security of healthy boundaries.

What puts the intuitive child at risk for shutting down when conflict arises? Well, the yelling, screaming, out-of-control anger that isn't resolving anything can be extra frightening to intuitive children because they often feel emotional conflict as real, physical experiences. If they experience loud, angry insults being hurled, it can create a violent, unsafe, and chaotic atmosphere. Angry blasts don't resolve conflict, and things are often said that people later regret. I recommend that when a couple identifies that their conflict is headed in this direction they take a time-out with an agreement to talk things out after they've cooled down.

Kids can benefit from seeing that their parents need to take time to cool down, too. If they are uncomfortable with the conflict that is still hanging in the air during the cooldown, remind them that it isn't their responsibility to fix the problem. If you have a child who prefers harmony, it might be hard for the child to let the conflict sit and get busy with something else. These children might benefit from doing a favorite activity that gets them back into their own "space" and untangled from your conflict. After you have cooled down and resolved the conflict, your child will see the value of your actions by noticing the peace that has been restored. Children don't need to know the content; they are just looking to make sure that their parents are connected with each other again.

When Intuitive Children Overuse Their Gifts to Take Care of Others

It is vital for intuitive children to learn that just because they can feel, sense, or have a big hunch about what another person is feeling, they don't have the responsibility to fix the perceived problem. It is important to teach them how to observe others without carrying the responsibility of healing. I can't tell you how much energy this viewpoint will save children over the course of their lives. All too often, intuitive types can be mistaken in the notion that if a dark emotion can be felt in someone else, it implies or invites the need to heal it. Intuitive children can also mistakenly think that if they intuit something troubling about a person's present or future circumstances that they have a responsibility to warn that person.

As an intuitive myself, I've often struggled with the complex issues of boundaries, integrity, and responsibility that come with the terrain of having intuitive messages float up for me. It can take a long time to find a comfort zone in knowing what calls for action and what is just something to observe and keep silent about. While children are learning about this process, it can be helpful for them to hear that they can share their intuitions with you freely and without judgment and that they aren't responsible for acting on the information. I see the relief on the faces of my adult intuitive clients all the time when they absorb this lesson.

Most children need support in learning how to deal with what it feels like to be in someone else's shoes. But intuitive children can be overloaded by the amount of data that comes in about other's people's feelings. This can lead to unique issues. They might shut down by becoming overwhelmed, or they might start to act out the feelings of the group or the person in need. Many times, their behavior is fueled by an unconscious desire or hope to create more harmony around them. In other words, "If I can help you to feel better, then I'll feel better, because I'm sensing you anyway!" Despite the problems that can emerge with this tendency, it may also be exactly what makes these children natural healers, fabulous communicators, and community activists. At its worst, it holds the risk of giving them the idea that they can only have peace if they control their environment by healing it or making it better. It is vital for children to learn that they can choose when to use their abilities. It is never their job to heal everything and everybody around them.

This particular dynamic can be especially slippery in the parenting relationship. Children are dependent on us daily and it is easier on them if we are happy and healthy. If children discover that they can use their gifts to cheer up a cranky mommy or daddy and that they then feel much better, it can be a tough cycle to break. The pairing of a positive result from your child's behavior with a feeling of personal relief begins to reinforce the behavior, and before you know it, the savvy, intuitive child is realizing that she can wield a unique power in the world. The trouble is that the child gets rewarded for thinking, "I'll be who you want or need me to be to meet your needs at the expense of mine." Practiced over time and without enough counterbalance of just being herself, the child's clear sense of self can become confused.

The antidote is to teach children to observe, not take on, the denser emotional states of sadness, grief, anger, and other upsets. Teach them how to bring a compassionate awareness to a situation without having to jump in and fix it. By all means, also let children know that it is their right to walk away whenever possible if something is overwhelming to them. Children can't always have a say in how much negativity they are exposed to, but they can learn that it is possible to practice making choices about how they will respond to that negativity. Children who are learning the power of this choice-making ability can observe a parent's low mood and say to themselves, "Wow, Dad's in a bad mood right now; I think I'll take some space," rather than, "I better get busy cheering Dad up so we can all feel better again."

✳ Amanda — age 6
Not Taking On Mom's Bad Mood

Intuitive Amanda felt quite safe setting her boundaries around negativity in her home. When her mom turned on the news, she'd call out, "Turn it off, turn it off!" Soon her mom began watching the news after Amanda's bedtime. This same child also gave her mom a terrific unspoken gift on a particularly "grumpy mom day." She chose to steer clear of her mom's mood by going into her room, closing the door, and making art for an hour. She emerged happy with her art creation and did a beautiful job taking care of herself by just taking some space and not by trying to fix her mom's mood.

Handling Sticky Situations Created by a Child's Telepathy

Intuitive children often catch their parents by surprise with their perceptions, leaving the parents wondering what to do next. The following story deals with the challenge faced when children ask questions to which they are not developmentally ready to hear the answer. The parent's task is to respond in a way that matches the child's emotional development.

✸ Michael — age 8

Tunes in to the Unspoken Family Secret

Michael was an amazingly bright, highly gifted intuitive boy. Many people who met him felt that he was an "old soul." Michael's parents came to see me for marriage and family counseling in the midst of a marriage crisis catalyzed by the surfacing of a long-held family secret. Michael had learned clues about the family secret but he knew no details. However, his intuitive empathy skills gave him specific details about it and he wanted to know if the adult-rated content was true. Michael's parents struggled to find a way to honor his intuition while also protecting him from information that could overwhelm an 8-year-old child. Together, we worked out a way to speak with Michael that acknowledged his feelings and hunches, but also reserved the right to privacy for his parents. In this way, his parents didn't have to lie to him and further confuse Michael. And Michael could have his feelings acknowledged with the added assurance that if this was still important to him in a few years, he could obtain more information. Verification of his feelings in this tricky situation had to be suspended, but not indefinitely. Michael felt acknowledged with this response, and his parents honored his perceptions even more deeply despite the pain triggered by his perceptive question.

In the next section, we turn the focus onto taking good care of the most important people in the highly intuitive child's life—the parents and caregivers.

How Your Own Intuition Can Help Your Parenting

Whether you are a highly intuitive parent or not, you can develop your own intuitive muscle to help you become more attuned to the needs of your child. Your intuition can be your greatest ally, not only in meeting your child's needs when tricky emotional and energetic experiences surface, but even in meeting the most basic of needs. Intuition is especially helpful when children don't yet have words for their experiences. For example, when you are parenting a baby you might have a feeling in your body corresponding to a need that the baby has, even before there is any external information (such as crying or a facial expression). Remember Christina in Chapter 1? Christina knew to respond to the needs of her cat's hunger when she felt the tickle in her stomach. Of course, the complexities of parenting and motherhood can hardly be compared to this small example, but, in truth, they are operating from a similar place of intuitive empathy.

You can improve your bearings on your own intuition by practicing one of the lessons that I recommend for the children: **knowing the difference between your energy and someone else's energy**. It is important to know how to distinguish your energy from someone else's energy because we need to have an anchor in taking care of our own body's needs and wants instead of reacting to whatever we might pick up on from those around us. If the aches and pains and feelings of those around you don't influence you, you may not need help developing this skill. But the unspoken feelings of your child may have more of an influence on your mood than you realize. Let's say that you were going along with your day and were in a happy mood. You've just picked up your child from school but haven't been with him for more than ten minutes, and suddenly you're exhausted. What's going on? It is possible that you're picking up on your child's exhaustion. When you check the data, sure enough your child is exhausted even though he isn't looking like it at the moment. Once you can differentiate that this physical feeling belongs to someone else (in this case, your child), you can make a choice about how to proceed instead of just succumbing to the feeling. As a parent you could process the child's exhaustion, find out how he got to that point, and make a plan for taking care of him that afternoon. Perhaps over the course of the afternoon, you might learn that your child took on the emotions of his classmates and a few conflicts at school that day. With the emergence of this new information about your child's day, you have the opportunity to harness a teachable moment for anchoring several of the ten skills. The next section of this chapter looks at how to keep intuitively clear by listening to your inner guidance and paying attention to your state of being.

listening to your inner guidance

One of the ways to harness our own intuition is to take some time to become internally quiet and ask the question, "How would my spirit guide me to act in this moment as a parent?" As we listen to that quiet, or perhaps loud, inner wisdom we will be guided to our next steps. If you are uncomfortable with the term *your spirit*, you can imagine this part as your wise self, your inner guide, or your inner resource expert. When you dial in your awareness to this uniquely insightful part of yourself, you might find that it simplifies decision making, greatly reduces mental processing time, and can help you achieve a perspective or solution that is right on track.

You can cultivate the ability to hear your inner voice as a parent by turning your attention inward on a regular basis throughout the day. It is difficult to hear your inner voice if you are stressed. One of the quickest and most obvious, but often forgotten, ways to reconnect to ourselves is to take several deep breaths. I like to close my eyes when I take these deep-breathing periods in order to give my eyes and senses a rest and to tune in to my body with greater ease. If I'm tense, it can be harder to hear my inner guidance. I've learned to try to stay present to the tension and not judge it. I use these times as an opportunity to be gentle with myself. For example, I can simply acknowledge that today has been tough and I'm doing the best job that I can.

As the mind and emotions calm down, it becomes easier to hear messages from our inner guidance. When you tune in to this wisdom place, it might feel as though you are making it up. This is normal. It will become clearer the longer you practice this tuning in to yourself. One of the ways that you can distinguish this wisdom voice from other feelings is that it always comes through with love. You may also feel lighter, more peaceful, and more hopeful about the situation at hand.

It is vital that you trust yourself when it comes to checking in with your inner guidance. The linear mind may want to launch into criticism, but keep in mind that as you follow the guidance of your wise voice, you can provide wonderful support to your intuitive child. It is never too late to fill in the gaps in our self-trust.

exploring self-trust

The following journaling questions can help you to explore your own level of self-trust:

★ *How are you doing in your life with regard to trusting yourself?*

★ *Do you respect the voice of wisdom within yourself?*

★ *Are you decisive about what matters most to you?*

★ *Are you in tune to what you need, and is the volume on your needs louder than what other people might be demanding from you?*

★ *If you had an even deeper trust in yourself, how do you think your life might or might not change?*

★ *Are you comfortable with speaking up for your own needs? Are you conveying the importance of listening deeply within and trusting yourself to your intuitive child?*

How Intuitive Children Respond to Parenting from the Heart

Parenting can sometimes feel like it takes the commitment of both a rigorous spiritual and physical practice. To keep up with these demands, where will you find your juice? What will help you to go the distance of the last two hours of the day when you're tired and in need of a break or when your child has just melted down? For me, the X ingredient is love. If you take one thing from this book, I would hope for it to be remembering to parent from your heart. Whenever we choose to parent from love, we add more positive energy to our child's energy bank and that of our shared relationships. It also cultivates a relational safety that is essential for the intuitive child.

Just hanging out in the feelings of the heart changes things—the feeling in a room, between people, our families, and within our own bodies. Recent scientific discovery lends itself beautifully to the practice of parenting from the heart. Research conducted by neurocardiologists indicates that 60 percent of the cells in our heart are neural cells—that is, the types of cells originally thought to exist only in the brain.[1] This finding teaches us that intelligence essentially does exist beyond our brains—in our hearts.

Parenting Based on Listening to and Respecting the Child

Many traditional parenting techniques teach us that as parents we hold the information our children need in order to maneuver through life and grow into responsible adults. Coming from this perspective, a child's hunches or insights would often not be taken seriously. In the case of parenting an intuitive, traditional parenting can be too controlling for the child's spirit. The reason for this is that assumptions are made, often unilaterally, based on the parent always knowing what is best for the child. I find that this old model isn't conducive to teaching intuitive children the ten skills they need to possess in order to thrive.

Alternatively, a parenting style that promotes respect for the child at its core fundamentally challenges old paradigms in raising kids. It shakes up the view of "I'm the parent and so I'm in charge and what I say goes. Period." It also challenges collective beliefs around the idea that "I am older; therefore, I am smarter than you are," and "You only get wise through life's lessons, and wisdom can only come after becoming an adult." Beliefs such as these don't allow room for a child's intuitive insights or hunches. A respectful parenting style tests the balance of power and invites a sharing of ideas, impressions, perspectives, and feelings from all family members. The new paradigm can look like this: "I'm the parent; therefore, it is my job to be with you in your daily life and to guide your development with as much love as I can harness moment to moment. I will treat you with care and respect and involve you in the decisions that impact your life as much as possible. I will listen to your feelings, respect your intuition, and help teach you how to use your gifts."

This stance doesn't say that the child is in charge and that you are off duty as a parent. After all, every child needs boundaries and leadership from parents in order to feel safe and to accomplish key developmental tasks held in common by all children, be they highly intuitive or not. I am in favor of deeply respecting our children and engaging in all the small and big ways we can use to meet their inherent needs with love and flexibility in the process. This model engages us as thoughtful and respectful guardians who respond to the needs of our children, adapting our parenting style based on what is needed at the time.

Some children, with the help of their intuition, may hold a piece of the puzzle for solving one of the world's biggest problems and may be destined to help the world in some big way. Why would we treat such a marvelously talented being with the disrespect that is found in the old model? And what if in practicing the old model of authoritative parenting, children were to become disconnected from the knowledge of their life's purpose? What if it meant that, because of this disconnection, children would end up spending years sorting out their truth as an adult before they could hit the deck running with their life's mission? Maybe, with a whole lot of love, the model of parenting based on deep respect for our children will help them stay connected to their inner wisdom and allow them a lifetime of growth and happiness, not a childhood from which they need to recover.

Being Kind to Yourself

No one is perfect and no one is a perfect parent. If we were stuck on the idea that we should be the perfect parent, imagine the stress this would cause sensitive intuitives. Not only would they pick up the underlying feeling, but maybe they would even receive an overt message that it is important to strive for perfection. This is a lot of pressure to put on ourselves, not to mention our children. How freeing it is for ourselves, and the people around us whom we love, to make peace with the reality that we will all make mistakes and it is oh so human. Children can benefit tremendously from seeing adults model humor and self-acceptance through their own mistakes.

It is helpful to be as kind and nonjudgmental with ourselves as possible when we take a look at the areas in our life that need improvement. When we meet our challenges with resistance, it can cause suffering and make it even harder to access and transform. A severe inner critic can create brittleness over time and reduce our flexibility. I've witnessed this phenomenon repeatedly in my work as a therapist, and I hope you'll give yourself the gift of gentleness with your own limitations. Your child is aware of you and what you project into the world, and your child will appreciate the soft heart that she sees you integrating as you learn about yourself.

chasing away guilt

Sometimes parents feel guilty when they take time out for themselves. I hope that you will be on the lookout for this draining emotion and if you catch its presence, choose to take care of yourself guilt-free like Ellie did.

✴ Ellie — age 38
Mother of Two Reclaims Taking Care of Herself

Ellie was a mom of two young children who were 3 and 6 years old, and she needed a break. Not the occasional kind, but the kind that she could build into her schedule every day. She loved her family tremendously, but the wear of being in service to them 24/7 had left her exhausted, frequently impatient, and resentful at times. The resentment alarmed her and was the wake-up call to make a change. Ellie dreamed of having more time every day and to regularly get out and go for a run on the beach near her home. She struggled with the details of how to make sure her children were taken care of while she took care of her own needs. Just when she felt the problem was insurmountable, she had an "aha moment." She realized that if she gave herself the permission to take this time, the details would fall into place. She had to be willing to claim this time for herself, guilt-free. It wasn't a selfish indulgence, but rather a vital part of her life and, in turn, her family's well-being. Child care soon fell into place, her husband was able to be a little more flexible with his work schedule, and soon her family was cheering her on as a new runner. Best of all, Ellie felt more energized, healthy, and patient. She rapidly transformed into a mother who was capable of giving, without the old resentments. Her children benefited from having their mom be present to them with love, without the tinge of resentment, and family life took on more of a sense of flow.

Being authentically kind and dropping the inner critic with ourselves as parents automatically puts us in the position of being an ally, not an adversary, to our needs. By listening deeply and intently to what we, ourselves, truly need, we can get busy with living the real deal. We can choose to take that nap, walk, speak the truth, say no, say yes, and be freed from the tyranny of doing things to please others and other games of the mind. You are worth this kindness right now, not in two weeks when you finish the to-do list. You are worth this right now. So go ahead and chase away the guilt, give yourself permission to take care of yourself, and just watch as everyone in the family benefits.

meditation on kindness

You can do this guided meditation by just reading it slowly and imagining giving yourself the gift of these suggestions as you read, by closing your eyes after a sentence or two and letting each part soak in, or by having a friend read it to you slowly, pausing after each sentence.

Begin by taking a few deep breaths. Breathe slowly and deeply into your abdomen, filling your lungs to capacity, and then very slowly exhale. Each time you exhale, you are letting go more and more. Do this ten times. Now, focus on your heart. Become aware of the ways in which you close your heart, through guilt, frustration, anger, fear, sadness, self-protection, or resentment. Breathe right into your heart. Relax into your heart. Slowly, let it soften. Now, imagine that you are surrounding yourself with the most exquisite kindness. Your body is relaxing into this space where you are truly free to be yourself, exactly as you are in this moment. This kindness whispers in your ear: Be yourself; you are enough. You are free to drink from this cup of kindness that life has poured out for you. It is an infinite supply. Please be generous with yourself. What would kindness choose for you in this moment? Is it kind to take a deeper breath, to take some space, to drop any concerns for just this moment? Listen to what next step toward being kind to yourself your intuition may be guiding you to. Return gently.

art exercise

Imagine that you have a cup inside of you and it is designed to hold kindness received both from others and yourself. How much can yours hold? Is the cup in any need of repair? What would it take to repair it? Are you prepared to have a cup that can receive to the point of overflowing? What would this look like?

teaching the ten skills

Education is not the filling of a pail,
but the lighting of a fire.

WILLIAM BUTLER YEATS

This chapter provides the ten skills highly intuitive children need for increasing their overall competency, reducing stress, and developing into balanced and secure adults. I came up with the concept of teaching these skills based on years of seeing common trouble spots in my intuitive clients. I soon realized that it was possible to teach a number of skills preventively and thus circumvent some of the stress and suffering that happens when intuitive and empathic input overwhelms a person.

The "How" Behind Teaching the Skills

Deciding when, where, how, and what to teach your child based on the suggestions contained in this chapter can be just as important as the skills themselves. In other words, the way in which you teach these skills, your own feelings and attitudes, and the particular context or situation in which you happen to be in with your child, all have an important impact on how your child will learn the skills.

Intuition isn't linear, and I find that teaching these skills doesn't always fall into a straight line. It isn't like teaching math. Although some of the skills are abstract, intuitive children, on a whole, tend to be pretty forgiving of being taught concepts that have a few details left out. They tend to fill in the missing pieces with their capacity for putting the bigger picture together. You can gauge whether or not these skills are actually benefiting your child by checking to see if they are actually making a difference and providing some relief in your child's life.

In my clinical practice, I teach these skills as the need arises, looking for those teachable moments when the window of opportunity opens and the skills can have a real impact. It will help to take note of the situations in which your child gets stuck and use these skills in a way that feels comfortable to you. For example, maybe your child routinely gets overwhelmed by picking up on other people's stress at the mall. This might be the real-life moment that will allow you to teach the skills of pulling in the antenna, getting grounded, or even visualizing the bubble of light.

I encourage you to tailor these skills to the unique needs of your child and your own personal style for delivering the information. You might even want to try the particular skills out yourself so you gain a better feel for the nuances of exactly what these skills can achieve. If you don't find the need for these skills in your own life because you aren't impacted by intuitive, empathic stress, you might find more of a need to elicit feedback from your child a bit more often so you know you are on a track that is truly helpful. The use of these skills might also feel a bit more foreign, imaginative, or even silly for some parents. I find that many sensate adults do not need to work as hard as do highly intuitive adults on skills such as grounding, setting emotional boundaries, and setting the more subtle energetic boundaries. Perhaps it may seem strange to need to teach a child something that you come by naturally. It might help to keep in mind that your own highly intuitive child may not come by these skills naturally and will need your help to develop them.

When to Teach the Skills

A child's personal development will significantly impact the timing of when you decide to teach these skills. I am intentionally leaving out age-specific recommendations for when and how to teach them because my experience has been that many of the skills can be taught to some children as young as 2 to 3 years old and not until school age with others. Keep in mind that these are children who have exceptional empathic mirroring capabilities, so if you are practicing these skills, chances are that your child may very well be picking up on them simply by observing how you feel and how you deal with situations. For example, if you want your child to become more grounded, make sure that you work on being grounded yourself and see if something positive shifts for your young child. The child could empathically mirror and internalize your sense of feeling calm and centered without even a word being said. As you both learn and teach these skills, you might find that you enjoy and benefit from the additional focus and commitment you make in modeling these skills for your child.

Understanding vs. Knowledge

In many of the Native American traditions, children are taught through stories that invite the child to contemplate lessons or truths in their own timing. According to Basil Johnston, author of *Ojibway Heritage,* "To foster individuality and self-growth, children and youth were encouraged to draw their own inferences from the stories. No attempt was made to impose specific views upon them. The learner learned according to his capacity. Each according to his gifts."[1] Malcolm Margolin sheds light on the concept of Indian pedagogy: "The knowledge and teachings you needed were not necessarily yours because you wanted them or even worked directly for them. Knowledge often came as a gift, and the goal of Indian pedagogy was to teach people the respect and alertness necessary so that they could recognize, receive, and, in the end, use the gifts that the world had given them."[2] I find that this style of teaching life's lessons is a beautiful match for teaching intuitive skills. The open-ended, child-centered, deeply respectful means of eliciting and supporting learning is a terrific backdrop for absorbing these lessons. This style also underscores the importance of creating opportunity for learning and understanding, rather than simply filling a child's mind with facts or more knowledge. This teaching style organically invites children to personally connect to the lesson instead of having it imposed on them. The result is that children often integrate these lessons deep inside instead of tucking them into the short-term memory bank. It is important for children to find their own personal meaning with these skills. Ideally, they will learn to deeply listen to and attend to all of their needs and discover far more skills than suggested within this book.

I recommend taking care to not set the bar of expectation too high for yourself or for your child with the proposed skill set. These skills can take a lifetime to master, as you'll hear more about in the final chapter concerning adult intuitives. Even if the skills aren't mastered by the time they leave home as young adults, the seeds for these skills will be planted and can be utilized at a time when they are ready.

SKILL NUMBER 1: *Learning How to Tell the Difference Between Random Fears and Intuition*

It is important to learn how to distinguish between an intuition and a random feeling or fear and then to practice acting on one's intuition.

In Chapter 2 you met Anna, the girl who had the intuitive hunch about the fugitive. Anna exercised great trust in her intuition when she insisted that her mom listen to her intuition about danger on their street and lock the doors. Her mom, on the other hand, was not certain that her daughter's feelings were based on a true intuition and understandably chalked it up to anxiety, imagination, and random fear. That story illustrated some of the ways to tell the difference between random fears and a true intuition about possible danger. As you may recall, when Anna received her intuitive hunch she experienced:

★ an abrupt change in mood with the incoming intuition

★ a feeling of danger in the body

★ a sense of immediacy

Most of us, whether highly intuitive or not, have had an intuitive, gut feeling of danger about a certain person or situation that proved to be accurate, even when there was no evidence. Highly intuitive children have this gut feeling more often than other people. Skill number one is both an awareness skill and an action skill. If your child has a hunch about danger, it is important to teach him to *act on it* in appropriate ways and also to *check for validity* whenever possible.

The ability to distinguish between anxious imagination and random fear is a skill that develops over time. Although it is not always easy to tell the difference, especially in children, each time an intuition is acted on and checked for validity, and it turns out to be right on, it strengthens the ability to determine a true intuition in the future. On the other hand, if intuitive hunches are not honored and no action is taken, there is a real danger that they will become entangled, lost, and indistinguishable from the realm of anxious imagination. Unfortunately, this happens far too often and becomes a tragic loss of such an important and helpful ability.

SKILL NUMBER 2: *Regulating the Intuitive Antenna*

Intuitive children are capable of gathering impressions, feelings, and even telepathic information from sources far and wide. In order to feel less bombarded or overwhelmed by the input from specific channels, it is important to learn how to regulate the intuitive antenna.

Highly intuitive children can get lost occasionally when they tune in to upsetting or conflicting intuitive channels. In Chapter 2 you met Kyle, the child who was upset by tuning in to the suffering of Africa's gorillas. Kyle's story illustrated several key ways in which the intuitive antenna can be regulated. When your child is feeling overwhelmed by a bombardment of intuitive information, it is important to be aware of the following:

★ Attend to the initial upset and help the child calm down.

★ Listen for evidence of the intuitive channel; see how far it extends.

★ Identify the particular concern.

★ Tailor your parenting response to the concern on that channel.

★ Break it down into a meaningful, child-friendly reality.

★ Make it tangible and take action if needed.

As you may recall from Kyle's story in Chapter 2, the previous points were linked with specific examples of what his parents were able to do to address his issue:

★ **Attended to the initial upset and helped the child calm down:** Kyle's parents provided immediate comfort and attentive soothing.

★ **Listened for evidence of the intuitive channel; found out what channel the information is coming in on:** His parents didn't initially know what the big upset was all about, but it emerged when Kyle started to give details and they could listen for how very far the channel reached (in this case, Africa).

★ **Identified the particular concern:** Kyle was worried about the gorillas in Africa.

★ **Tailored their parenting response to the specific concern:** Kyle needed help addressing his specific concerns once they emerged clearly.

★ **Broke it down into a meaningful, child-friendly reality:** Kyle and his parents researched organizations that help the gorillas in Africa.

★ **Made it tangible and took action:** Making the donation empowered Kyle because he could do something to help.

deep breathing and mindfulness as a way of pulling in the antenna

When highly intuitive children are feeling anxious or upset because of an intuitive hunch, it is important not to immediately discount their fears as mere imagination. After first listening to the content of their concerns, help them settle back into themselves comfortably. Soothing an upset child with calm, attentive parenting can take many forms. One way to do this is to take a few deep breaths with your child. Some children will balk at this seemingly silly activity, but we all know how to breathe, and even very young children can be reminded to take nice, slow, deep breaths. I recommend that parents do the exercise with their children because as children hear and feel a parent's deep breathing, they will likely mirror that sense of relaxation and comfort in themselves. It is very difficult to remain stressed while taking slow, deep breaths and paying attention to the here and now. You can hold the child on your lap or sit side-by-side, depending on your child's comfort level. If you can separate yourself from the bustle of a busy household for a few minutes to do this, I recommend this additional level of quiet.

Older children and teens can take this technique a step further by practicing pausing between the in-breath and the out-breath. The additional pause for mindfulness helps to turn down the volume on intuitive input by bringing focused awareness to the moment of that breath. Focusing on breathing, and even the isolation of the in-breath from the out-breath, slows down our awareness and pulls awareness into subtle perceptions at the physical level, which in turn pulls in the intuitive antenna.

visualization: another technique for pulling in the antenna

Another technique for calming down and pulling in the antenna involves imagination. Have children imagine that they literally have an antenna on their heads (or somewhere on their bodies where they feel it most). Ask them to get a sense of how it feels to be picking up on so much information. Now have them imagine they are slowly pulling the antenna in, closer and closer to their bodies, making the antenna shrink smaller and smaller until it is just a little dot. You can further support this skill by having the children draw a picture of what it feels like to have their antenna system in the "on" and "off" positions. Remind them that this is part of how they learn to turn off the switch from all of those big feelings and intuitions. It is their right to turn it off if they need a break, and it can be very empowering for them to know they can exercise personal choice in where they put their focus.

SKILL NUMBER 3: *Turning the Volume down on the Intuitive Dial*

Highly intuitive children need to know how to turn their attention away from other people, events, and environments to go deep within themselves. They need to learn how to turn down the volume on their intuitive input. In this way, children know they can have a break from the intense stimuli in the environment around them and in the world.

Although there are some parallels between skill number two—regulating the antenna system—and skill number three—turning down the volume on the intuitive dial—the skills are different. Whereas regulating the antenna has to do with picking up on information in specific channels and identifying it, turning down the dial involves a more general ability to regulate intuitive stimuli coming in from all directions.

The ability to turn the volume down on the intuitive receiver is one of the most important skills a sensitive, intuitive person can learn. As with so many of the skills I teach in this book, this one will likely take well into adult life to fully master. It is an essential skill because without it intuitive children stand the risk of being overstimulated by the amount of intuitive information they receive. If children know that they have the tools to help calm their minds, emotions, and bodies, it won't be quite as scary, tiring, or overwhelming.

When children come to an adult because they are overwhelmed by an intuitive upset, it can be tempting to launch straight into helping them get their mind off what is upsetting them, but this bypasses an essential step. The first thing to do is to listen to the child and learn more about why she is upset and what is being communicated in the intuitive message. How does it make her feel? What is your child noticing about the sensations in her body? What does she think the intuition is all about? As you listen to your child and perhaps offer soothing words or other forms of comfort, you can listen for all the different layers of information. You might hear clues about the channel of intuition she is picking up on (like family, friends, or the world), or maybe she had a tough experience at school and can't let go of wondering about the welfare of a buddy. Whatever it is, there may be an important story that needs to be witnessed by a loving, interested adult. The simple act of having our true experiences heard without judgment can be very comforting. You might even find that simply listening at the time solves the issue of turning down the volume.

When we support children in turning down the volume on their intuitive feeling input, we are helping them calm down at the mind, body, and spirit levels. The following ideas are designed to help calm down states of arousal and reestablish balance in the child:

★ **Encourage physical activity and exercise:** Exercise helps to increase levels of endorphins that reduce stress and increase a feeling of well-being in the body. Exercise brings more oxygen to the brain, connects children with the here and now, and can help take them out of any kind of mental loop they might be stuck in. Exercise is all about being in the body and has a direct correlation with bringing the volume down in a child-friendly fashion.

★ **Turn on some music or an audio story:** Children who "hear" intuitive input may be especially comforted by having this channel of information temporarily suspended by having something else to listen to. Listening to music, lyrics, or a recorded story disrupts them from the volume of their own intuitive story and can give it a rest. If the music or story is uplifting, your child is also taking in a positive "diet" input for his spirit at the same time.

★ **Focus on the here and now:** As with skill number two, coming back to the here and now is a great way to turn down the volume. Focusing on the gentle rhythm of the breath, counting breaths slowly, or paying close attention to all the details of a flower, a bug, or the sounds of water or music can all help in coming back to the present and turning down the dial. One popular Buddhist meditation on mindfulness involves eating just one raisin very, very slowly and noticing everything you can about that raisin. Whether it is a raisin or a piece of chocolate, mindfulness can be a great way of supporting awareness of the here and now.

★ **Release the hook:** If your child's temperament is such that there is a tendency toward certain emotional issues such as anxiety or depression, she may be more sensitive to picking up on these very same things in the environment and in other people. This sensitivity creates an emotional resonance and an intuitive "hook" that makes children more vulnerable to picking up on the feelings of other people who have similar issues to their own. The result can be an extra dose of the anxiety. When a child is picking up on someone else's feelings because they are similar in nature to what the child feels emotionally, it can make for a confusing mix. In this instance, the question "Is this mine or yours?" can be frustratingly muddled. Turning down the volume in these instances usually means helping children deal with their own preexisting feelings. Once children who tend toward anxiety learn the skills necessary to help manage their worries, they are less likely to be a magnet for picking up on and carrying other people's worries around with them. The result is that they release the hook.

★ **Give your attention and intention to staying balanced and enjoying life:** Have you ever noticed that when you are feeling strong, happy, and at peace with yourself you are less likely to be thrown off balance by other people's problems? The same is true for children. Making pleasure, fun, and balance priorities is vital for intuitive children so that they stay resilient and less likely to feel the burdens of others. Focusing on having a fun break is a great way to bring down the volume on upsetting input.

★ **Take the "over" out of the equation:** Because of their ability to not only pick up on what other people are feeling, but to also feel deep empathy, highly intuitive children tend to bend over backward in an effort to respond to the distress around them. This can cause a lot of stress and suffering for them. Listen for evidence that your child is overfunctioning in some way by overcaring, overresponding, over-reaching, or any other way that the child is giving more than is appropriate in a situation, especially if it is causing the child stress. Remind children that their job is to be themselves and that they don't have to work so hard at taking care of everybody else. The ability of perceptive intuitive children to tune in to the needs of those around them does not translate into a responsibility to do something about it.

SKILL NUMBER 4: *Cultivating an Intuitive Vocabulary*

It is important for parents and children to develop a vocabulary for speaking about their unique needs and experiences, and to know how to find people who can be supportive of their intuitive abilities.

The primary means of expression within modern culture is through words, and it can be hard to pair words with intuitive experiences. This difficult intersection can result in a feeling of being misunderstood in intuitive kids. Part of the problem lies in not having a common lexicon. As adults we can help intuitive children begin to develop a vocabulary for their experiences. This is important because these words then act as a bridge to let you know when they need your help or protection. It also provides a common ground for understanding and talking about these kinds of unique feelings and invisible hunches.

Vocabulary development for intuitive experiences happens in a few different ways. Body signals are key and often inspire the kinds of descriptors that a child will use. Therefore, many of the words for this intuitive vocabulary will likely describe how intuitive experiences affect the physical body—or how empathic information is felt in the child's body. Examples of children making the connection between physical sensations and words include, "That man made my body feel prickly and cold all of a sudden," or "My body feels so heavy and sad when I enter that building."

When children speak these sensations out loud, take the time to truly hear what they are saying and ask to hear more about the feelings.

Each time children practice listening to their body sensations and then tune into the information that these feelings offer, they build their self-trust, self-awareness, and intuitive discernment abilities.

The following are some specific examples for helping your child develop an intuitive vocabulary in key areas:

For safety: When children are in a situation that doesn't feel safe intuitively, they will often use words and phrases such as "creepy," "skin crawling," "icky feeling in my stomach," or even "nauseous." You may want to agree on words, or some other kind of signal, that your child can use to communicate to you when she feels an intuitive sense of danger.

For empathic overload: When intuitive children feel overloaded by other people's emotions, words and phrases such as "I'm not feeling myself," "I'm sad and I don't know why," "All of a sudden I felt stressed (or a headache, or stomach ache, or tight inside)" may be used after they are around certain people. One boy described his empathic stress by saying, "I feel slumpish." Variations of "slump" became the common word in his family for describing this kind of emotional overload.

For making a decision: When children have a positive intuitive feeling about a certain situation or possible decision, the feeling could be described as "happy," "light," "bubbly," "peaceful," or "calm." On the other hand, if they feel intuitively negative about a situation or possible choice, they may use words such as "blocked," "tight," "tired," or "confused."

There are many other situations in which there will be a need to develop a vocabulary based on your child's intuitive experiences. As you pay attention to the words your child uses, offer suggestions, and develop a common language together, you will be helping your child to feel more deeply connected and understood.

Vocabulary related to intuitive and empathic experiences does have its limitations, though. In fact, many intuitive people often complain of the limiting nature of words when they are trying to express the details of an intuitive experience because linguistic specifics and intuitive pictures and general impressions can be a poor match. Giving words to intuitive experiences requires something akin to language translation skills that develop over time. When we translate a passage from one language into another, something is often lost in the translation. The same can be said for giving words to intuitive experiences. This is where the creative process can be a real lifesaver for intuitive children who want to express what they are feeling. It can give them a chance to express images from deep within that may be hard to give words to. The additional vocabulary of art, such as drawing, painting, poetry, and sculpture allows children to share with others some of the places that they travel to in their empathic experience.

It is also important to cultivate friendships where children feel comfortable being authentic. If you have a highly intuitive child, you may be lucky enough to know other children with similar tendencies. Friendships and groups of like-minded children, whether formal or informal, can be an extremely valuable support.

SKILL NUMBER 5: *Paying Attention to What You Want and Need*

Intuitive, empathic kids are very adept at perceiving and responding to other people's needs, and it is essential to counterbalance this tendency by having them pay close attention to their own needs, speaking up for these needs, and cultivating a lifelong practice of taking great care of themselves.

All children, of course, have needs. But intuitives have unique needs that are often overlooked. Many of the unique needs intuitives have tend to include:

- ★ dealing with sensitive body needs (Chapter 5)
- ★ reducing empathic stress (Chapter 3)
- ★ intuitive boundaries (Chapter 6)
- ★ counterbalancing their heightened awareness of other people's needs

The most important part of this skill is to help children develop an awareness of the signals that occur inside of them when there is a need that should be addressed. Through conversations with children about their specific needs, they will be able to internalize this awareness and draw upon it throughout their lives. The more children can honor their unique needs and take action to meet these needs on a daily basis, the higher the likelihood that they can stay happy, balanced, and emotionally clear.

Socially, it might be a challenge for highly intuitive children to take care of their needs. They are typically very perceptive of how other people experience them. They notice the slightest grimace that a friend gives when they pull out their extra nutritious lunch, or the quizzical passing look that two friends give each other when they overhear this child's mom overriding a play date offer because she sees how her child's nerves are starting to fray. Your child might want to be like the other kids, eat like the other kids, and keep up with the activity load of other kids. They might struggle with how tuning in to and taking care of their needs looks quite different from other children's needs. And in an attempt to fit in, they might naturally override those needs as they bump into the limits of what they can and cannot do. Criticisms for this child's sensitivities can arise among peers, siblings, extended relatives, and even well-meaning parents. And the sensitive, empathic, intuitive child is listening.

If your child is struggling with not wanting to appear or even feel different, you can explain that we are all different and differences need to be respected in life. When intuitive kids respect themselves, even as a minority group on the playground, they are more likely to take great care of themselves—even when you aren't around.

You can support your child by reminding him of how vital it is to listen to his needs and act on them. Keep the tone positive. Be especially on the lookout for the times when your child will all too easily forego what he honestly wants in order to appease you or others. You might hear comments like, "It's okay, Mommy, I didn't really want to do that," or "My friends would have been too upset if I'd done what I wanted." Children who are especially empathic will likely need extra help with this skill because they run a bigger risk of trying to meet the needs of others that they empathically feel—at the cost of taking care of themselves. This is a natural empathic tendency, and you can gently help steer your child back to healthier, self-nurturing decisions by reminding him to check in about whether or not he feels comfortable with things like changing his mind when others ask something of him. Is your child overriding a personal truth to avoid interpersonal discomfort? If so, this child may also need comforting and reassurance from you that it is okay to speak up for what he needs, even if it upsets or creates an inconvenience for others. This concept can appear foreign and cause a real struggle for the perceptive child. If you are not highly empathic yourself, you might also become frustrated because your child can't be more assertive and blurt out what he wants like other children. It is not that your child is incapable of those behaviors; he may simply be struggling with letting his needs supercede what he perceives to be the loudest needs in a given situation and that may often be someone else's.

If you find yourself frequently teaching your child this principle, know that you aren't alone and this particular skill can take extra time to learn for highly empathic children. You are teaching your child to soften an instinct for being highly aware of what other people need, and helping her turn that perceptive awareness around to taking good care of herself. In doing so, you won't rob your child of keen interpersonal instincts. You will be helping her learn to stand up for who she is, what she needs, and how to balance this with what other people want of her.

SKILL NUMBER 6: *Practicing Daily Energy Hygiene*

Intuitive children need to know how to clear out the feelings that they might have taken on during the day so that they don't feel depleted by these feelings or start to act them out.

We all know the importance of teaching children to wash their hands after using the toilet and before they eat a meal. We can't see the germs but we know they exist, so we practice good common sense by taking care of our bodies. Hygiene is important for our health, and it extends to our energy field as well. Although we can't prove it in a petri dish, *energy pollution* can have a real impact. For intuitive children, it is critical that they be taught the skills to clear their energy field of any unwanted energy pollution they may have picked up throughout the day. This pollution could include negative feelings and stress arising from other people and the environment. Just as good physical hygiene requires washing away invisible microorganisms with hand washing, good energy hygiene for intuitive, empathic children means finding a way to wash away invisible feelings and stressors they can pick up in the course of a day. Another way to think of this practice is that you'll be teaching your child to take out the "trash," so the trash basket doesn't overflow and make a big mess. The trash consists of those upsets that highly intuitive, empathic children observe and vicariously take on from outside. If these aren't released, the stress can overflow like the overflowing trash basket.

Many highly intuitive people jump to the conclusion that when they take on someone else's issues it is simply their own feeling, and they never consider that they are mirroring the other person. It is understandable that a child would believe that the emotion belongs to them. As we explored in Chapter 3, recent discoveries in neurobiology present evidence for a person's ability to create biological synchrony (i.e., "sync up") with another human being (mirror neurons). This can be a true gift if the exchange is a loving one. But when the syncing up proves to be negative, it can be immensely helpful for them to let it go and move on. Once the lousy feeling takes over in an uncomfortable exchange, it can be hard to practice energy hygiene. But this is just when it is vital to take action.

Some of the most common complaints I hear from intuitive people are feelings of being "off" and not comfortable in their own skin as a result of being particularly susceptible to other people's moods. I often find that these clients are having trouble releasing other people's energy. After repeatedly noticing this problem coming up, it became highly apparent that most people are not taught the importance of energy hygiene.

When clients learned the basics of energy hygiene, tailored to their own emotional and physical constitution, their energy and mood improved dramatically. I believe that energy hygiene is not an esoteric secret, but an essential, practical, must-have skill for highly intuitive children. This skill can also be approached in a matter-of-fact and fun manner without ever even having to deal with the complexities of terms like *energy hygiene*. In fact, it may be easiest to frame this skill for young children by saying something such as, "We are going to play our game of letting go of the day," and then moving on to the suggestions in the list below.

The basic premise of this skill is clearing and cleaning out the feelings your child might have picked up from other people, places, or situations. When an intuitive child has absorbed the feelings of another person or a situation to a significant degree, it can be hard to differentiate the cause. The cause may or may not be important to figure out, but helping your child let go of the stressors that were accidentally picked up from others is essential.

seven ways to squeeze out your energy sponge (for children)

The following techniques are designed to help highly intuitive and empathic children, those who absorb the feelings of other people like a sponge, squeeze out that sponge in a light and fun way.

1. HOOT into a pillow with big, wild movements.

2. SHAKE it off with your arms or to music of the child's choice.

3. BANG it into some clay—squeeze the clay, hammer it, rip at it, and put some mojo into it.

4. SCRUB it off with some water. Hop in the tub, shower, sprinkler, and maybe add some sea salt to help move things along.

5. BREATHE a few deep breaths together to get back to center after the bigger feelings have been expressed.

6. IMAGINE a color of safety and protection all around your child. Check to see if your child can feel his own energy again.

7. SEND a kind wish for balance and healing to all involved and see each person free and disconnected from the situation.

Here are shortcut tips for parents:

For anger: Steps 1, 2, and 3

For sadness: Try steps 4 and 5

Need to go straight to calming down: Steps 5 and 6

anchoring the energy hygiene skill

One of the ways you can help anchor this skill for a lifetime is to help your child grow accustomed to checking in with herself to see if there is anything that she needs to let go of. Bedtime can be an excellent time of day to ask your child to tune in to this need, but ideally, a child should also cultivate the ability to ask, "Is there something that I need to let go of?" earlier in the day if they are suddenly feeling disbalance. Energy hygiene is nothing new, but naming it and practicing it daily might feel new and different. Once you get the hang of it, it is not so mysterious.

In the Jewish tradition of Shabbat, a portion of this weekly Friday night ritual is devoted to hand washing, which symbolically washes away and helps the person let go of anything that is causing internal stress from the week. Sometimes families practice this portion of the ritual by speaking these concerns out loud to be symbolically released in the water. Throughout time and across human culture, we have evidence of the importance of washing energies away that are no longer ours to carry. Children who see adults "washing away" their worries and stress learn that this is a natural part of life.

The ancient Japanese practice of the daily ritual bath, or *ofuro*, is another cultural example of practicing daily energy hygiene. Before there was plumbing available for individual homes, families would gather at community-style hot baths in the evening. Today, many Japanese families have their own ofuro tubs and the ofuro is more than an opportunity to get clean. It signifies a time to let go of the day's concerns, to relax and prepare for a night of good rest. I'll never forget my own experience as an exchange student living in Japan and enjoying a soak in the largest family bathtub I had ever seen. I was so moved to feel the family rhythm created by everyone taking his or her turn with an ofuro soak at night. Clearly, the amount of space dedicated to the ofuro room and the time dedicated to this practice in the routine of life spoke to its cultural and family value.

Sensitive, intuitive children are born with the ability to naturally absorb and take in remarkable amounts of subtle information about people and life. For those times when they don't naturally release it on their own, they will need the help of learning how to let go of this excess information and these feelings so they don't become overwhelmed. Teaching them how to practice energy hygiene is a powerful step in that direction.

SKILL NUMBER 7: *Staying Grounded*

It is important for the child to feel safe and connected to the earth.

Grounding is basically a technique of stabilizing awareness in the here and now. Many spiritual traditions have spoken of the importance of grounding to create a sense of peace, health, and protection. Visualization works well for children who are learning the skills of grounding.

Have your child imagine that his body is connected to the core of the earth through either a magic cord that extends from the base of the spine or, if standing up, through roots extending down from the bottoms of the feet. You might have your child imagine the body as a tree with the roots penetrating deep into the ground (hence, grounding). You can take your guided imagery for the child further by reminding him to allow the ground to give him love, protection, and safety.

other fun ways of supporting grounding in children

Here are some additional easy ways to support grounding:

- ✶ camping, gardening, mud and dirt play, spending time playing outside

- ✶ time spent on land experiences and around bodies of water: lakes, oceans, rivers, streams, and even swimming pools or the bathtub

- ✶ any form of dance

- ⋆ sitting with a child's back up against a large tree trunk or climbing trees

- ⋆ playing with clay (natural clay is preferable to synthetic clays)

- ⋆ playing a musical instrument or rhythmic drumming

- ⋆ rubbing your child's feet or giving the child a back rub

keeping two feet in the here and now

Counterbalancing the power of intuitive leaps of time and understanding with a solid footing in the here and now is essential for highly intuitive children. Once people feel safe and grounded in their bodies, they are better prepared for experiencing the accelerations of understanding common to intuitives. A deep foundation for grounding in oneself is developed by practicing grounding skills and through establishing solid relationships and healthy self-esteem. If a child doesn't feel comfortable and successful as a person, there is little foundation for the benefits of staying grounded in the body. This is a process that grows over the span of a child's development. A simple way of looking at this process involves using the ABC acronym standing for: **A**cceptance, **B**elonging, and **C**onnection.

A for Acceptance means that children accept and value themselves. Over the course of their life experiences, children can create a storage bank of positive associations that add up to the feeling of competency in their life. Life doesn't have to be a total struggle. Instead, children can take the difficulties of life and work to find solutions and discover inherent strength. Highly intuitive children should be encouraged to feel that their different ways of looking at life are valuable and nothing to be ashamed of. They can feel at peace within themselves and learn to not judge personal mistakes harshly. Much of this skill can be fostered in the parenting relationship when we model it for our children. As we accept our children, they learn to accept themselves. When highly intuitive children are connected to positive self-esteem, it helps their sense of physical and emotional well-being and promotes grounding.

B for Belonging means that children know they belong here in life. Although this concept may seem obvious, intuitive children can sometimes struggle with feeling that they do not "belong" among people who do not possess the same highly intuitive and empathic abilities. They often wonder why other people don't see and feel life the same way they do, and they might feel as if they are from another planet. Many are also naturally very spiritual, and in some ways they may feel more connected to and familiar with an inner spiritual world rather than the physical world. We can help children who have these spiritual experiences by being willing to listen to these experiences and yearnings, and by reminding them of how much they matter in life and how they do "belong" here: in the family, community, and world.

C for Connection means that children grow in their awareness of being grounded through safe and loving relationships in their lives. Because highly intuitive children often feel as if they are from somewhere else, a deep sense of connection with others is essential. Given their unusual ways of perceiving life, which thus makes them feel different from others, having people in their lives who understand, accept, and positively affirm all the aspects of who they are is immensely helpful. This connection also allows them to feel more socially successful with friends and peers, whether those friends are highly intuitive or not.

A good, strong connection to the earth, to close relationships, and to the rhythm of life all contribute to a sense of grounding in the intuitive child. This sense of grounding contributes to the intuitive child feeling safe and connected in life, allowing the child to enjoy the gifts of intuition, as well as to be fully successful in the practical world.

SKILL NUMBER 8: *Distinguishing Your Energy from That of Others*

It is important for children to know where their own energy ends and someone else's energy begins. They can become familiar with asking, "Is this feeling mine, or does it belong to someone else?"

The parent-child relationship is a great place to start to teach the skill of how to distinguish one's own energy from that of someone else's, also known as *energetic differentiation*. If you spot your child starting to mirror your own emotional state (especially if it isn't a pleasant one), see if you can help your child to get clear about what is going on with her feelings. Here is how to do this:

★ First ask your child to check in with his body and ask what he is noticing.

★ Let your child know it is fine to share anything with you, including those things the child thinks might upset you. Feeling safe is essential to helping your child relax into this exercise. Your child needs to know it is perfectly all right to open up.

★ Next, direct your child to tune in to her feelings and ask, "Is this your feeling or do you think it might belong to someone else?" For example, if you were feeling particularly worried and suddenly your child was mirroring this emotion, you could be more specific and ask, "Is this feeling yours, or does it seem like you picked it up from me?" You might even venture deeper by personally sharing, "I was just feeling anxious a moment ago and then I noticed you starting to feel worried and upset. Do you think it's possible that you were picking up on my feelings?" If the answer is affirmative, it is a fine opportunity to remind the child that she doesn't need to absorb your feelings. Lovingly remind your child to let the feelings go. These techniques will simply help the child shift emotional direction, without having it be a mental exercise. When children are too young to understand the concept of differentiating energy, it is most helpful to simply have them do an activity that will naturally help them make the shift and let go of whatever feeling they may have taken on.

If children are able to make the distinction that the feeling belongs to someone else, bravo! They are mastering one of the most important skills for intuitive empaths: to be able to detect if what they are experiencing originated in their own body/mind system or if they are picking it up from someone else. Once children know that a particular feeling came from someone else, they can make a decision. They can actively choose to let it go—I find this is very liberating to children and adults alike, knowing they don't have to carry the burdens of other people on their own shoulders. If you find that your child has difficulty with learning this skill, know that the child is in good company.

Many adults work hard at mastering this skill. As an intuitive person, the question "Is this mine?" is one of my all-time favorites. It gets me focused on energetic boundaries and saves countless hours grieving over something that was never mine in the first place. It doesn't rob me of my empathy. Rather, it puts me in the empowered position of being able to be with someone else's pain because I am clear about my boundaries and can show up with compassion. In this way, I can choose to be with suffering and bare witness to it, rather than just absorb the pain of another person or group of people.

Once children can clarify whether they are dealing with their own feelings, or those that they picked up from someone else, they can move on to taking action, if needed. A simple question to ask is, "What do I need to do here, if anything?" This question helps to clarify if any action is necessary to keep their boundaries intact, even if it means excusing oneself from a conversation, game, or room.

SKILL NUMBER 9: *Handling Faulty Intuitive Conclusions/Checking Facts*

Intuitive leaps can sometimes be faulty and can be driven by imagined meanings, where none exist. Intuitive children often need help remembering to engage their rational, fact-finding skills to check out their intuitive conclusions. This skill helps in reducing anxiety and interpersonal stress associated with faulty intuitive leaps.

Because intuitive conclusions happen so quickly, they regularly bypass linear sequential logic. Einstein's intuitive leap to capture the theory of relativity, discussed earlier, is an example of positive intuition at work. He leaped out to his conclusion and then worked backward to fill in the details. Not every intuition needs to be backfilled in this way, but many do, so it is useful to know how this works. One excellent reason for mastering this skill is because sometimes the process of leaping to conclusions can backfire by giving a child faulty information. Therefore, it is important to help children learn how to check the facts and evaluate their conclusions. Learning how to engage both our intuitive and our logical "muscles" is vital to taking full advantage of our human capacities.

Teaching intuitive children the value of working backward to check conclusions can be an important life skill. Two typical areas where this challenge often shows up include relationships and specific fears. Let's take relationships first. A classic misfiring of intuition is the old "She's upset with me; I can just tell." In this situation, a child comes into contact with a friend who is in a bad mood and the child mistakenly assumes that the bad mood has something to do with her. Although the child sees and may even physically feel her friend's bad mood, the link to what has caused this feeling is not necessarily accurate. The intuitive child registers the feeling of upset in a friend and assumes it is her fault, but the missing link is the specific details or storyline about why the friend is upset. The other person's frustration may have absolutely nothing to do with the child who is noticing the mood. Have children check their intuitive leap with questions such as, "Are you mad at me, or could it be about someone else?" or "Do I actually *know* for a fact that this person is mad at me?" Be aware of children who repeatedly jump to conclusions that other people's bad moods are their fault. Help your child work backward to check the facts and not assume that other people's moods are her responsibility.

Another area for fact-checking is the big, scary world of fears. General worry is completely different from the crisp, well-defined intuitive message of needing to get out of a dangerous situation, as we saw in Chapter 2. Worries pull our attention out into the future and hold the mind hostage to the land of what-ifs. Intuitive children can be prone to worries for many reasons, as you learned in Chapter 4. When they worry, they project their attention toward a possible problem in the future, missing out on enjoying their life in the present moment. When a child makes an intuitive leap that turns into worry, this is an opportunity to employ the rational side of their brains. You can help them do this by encouraging them to play detective and check the facts about their fearful conclusions. Help them work backward to see what evidence supports their conclusions. Doing so encourages a balance between the rational and the intuitive and is great practice for an intuitive child. Best of all, it can greatly help in reducing their upsets concerning troubling worries.

Helping a highly intuitive child learn to confirm their impressions through facts and logic has its place in balanced child development. Each time an impression is confirmed, it strengthens their confidence and ability to recognize the difference between true intuition and imagination, fear, or anxiety.

SKILL NUMBER 10: *Incorporating Intuitive Empathy into Everyday Life*

Intuitive children need to integrate the trait into a healthy sense of self as they mature.

Over time, as the other nine skills are developed, an anchoring of the intuitive channels within the body, mind, emotions, relationships, and tasks of daily life will grow. As the highly intuitive child matures, the roots of physical and emotional security will nourish the blossoming of intuition in a balanced and beautiful way.

As I pointed out in Chapter 1, being highly intuitive and empathic isn't something that a child chooses—it is what he is born with. As children learn how to work with the possible challenges associated with high intuition and gain competency in these areas, they increase self-esteem associated with the trait. The result will be feeling comfortable in living with a sensitive, empathic, and intuitive system.

As poet William Bulter Yeats recommends, "Education is not the filling of a pail, but the lighting of a fire." Peace and competency with this trait won't come by merely filling a child's pail with the knowledge of these skills and ideas. Gradually, practicing and living these skills in life lights the fire of understanding and appreciation for these gifts, allowing intuitive children to live with respect for the gifts and fostering an openness to share them in the world.

art, play, and spirit
for the intuitive child

I'd rather make art than eat; it's so much fun!

ANONYMOUS INTUITIVE CHILD, AGE 3

I n this chapter, we will look at some of the most powerful tools for keeping life in balance for an intuitive child: art, play, and connecting to their own spiritual nature. These three areas are highlighted because they can be a reservoir of comfort, guidance, and support on the child's terms. Each one of these areas represents an inner resource that children can draw from over the course of their lives for balance, pleasure, creativity, guidance, transformation, healing, and connection. And while they are busy having fun and expressing themselves, they'll be learning even more about reducing stress, pulling in their intuitive antenna, getting rid of unwanted empathic feelings from others, and expressing their own personal preferences. Perhaps I'm biased to the gifts of art and play as an art therapist, but I can think of few other experiences in the life of a highly intuitive child that offer this much promise.

Why Support Art and Play?

The arts and a spirit of playfulness are enormously important in children's lives and an essential ingredient in supporting balance in an intuitive child. Creative arts and play naturally act to release the feelings and

143

impressions that intuitive children pick up from other people, whether it is in a paint-filled brushstroke, a loud thump on the drum, or a demonstrative leap of dance. Acts of creativity move energy, opening a flow of feelings and healing.

When intuitive children become burdened by seeing or feeling the intense pain and needs of others and even the world, they need a way to shake off what doesn't belong to them and process that information. The creative arts and play can be highly effective in helping with this process. No matter how verbally skillful we may be as parents, teachers, or therapists, children still need ways to process what life dishes out in their own time and way. The arts and play give the space and the means to do this. Anyone who has ever witnessed an upset child take flight to his art materials, linger over an art creation, and later emerge centered and balanced, knows the truth of this firsthand.

Let's look at Sophie's story, for example.

✳ Sophie — age 5
Using Art to Work Through Her Grief

When Sophie learned that her dog had been hit and killed by a car, the first thing she did was run inside the house to her painting easel. As her small body heaved with tears over the loss of her best pal, she painted and painted. Her parents stood close by but didn't interfere. They waited and watched as the sobs turned to sniffles and the painting began to slow down in its intensity. After about thirty minutes, Sophie reemerged, centered and calm. She gave them each a hug and walked away. She found her grief counseling in her paint pots that day, and her parents learned firsthand the power of art to heal.

I have spent most of my adult life witnessing the healing power of art and play in children's lives. The transformative power of art never ceases to amaze me. Art moves stuck emotional states, supports the experience of flow and ease, works out unconscious inner conflicts, and even stimulates the production of endorphins for stress relief. If that isn't reason enough to commit to more art and play, consider that it also builds self-esteem, inner balance, and exercises multiple human senses and systems simultaneously. It might just be one of the simplest, cheapest, and important facets of a child's happy development.

Another reason I am a fan of the arts for children is that it lets us off the hook as parents to have to be there with the perfect intervention (as if there ever was one!). Instead of turning to us for answers, children can express their own truth and we can stand back and function as facilitators and witnesses. What generally emerges when children are permitted the chance to honestly express themselves is the wisdom of their own inner guidance—as was the case when Sophie's dog died.

Art and play are terrific, child-friendly ways of supporting intuitive children in paying attention to their own likes, dislikes, boundaries, and understanding of their own sense of self, separate from the feelings and thoughts of others. This critical awareness is vital for the intuitive, empathic child who so easily tunes into the wants of others. Art and play invite a child into the direct experience of inner knowing, following instincts, and even stimulating the body's innate balancing system. Art also brings children back to their own experience of the here and now, allowing them to be receptive to their own ideas and feelings that spring from deep within. Again, this benefits the intuitive child who may be processing information that is future-related and distracting.

Words can be helpful, but highly intuitive children can greatly benefit from other ways of expressing their intuitive experiences. While I encourage the development of an intuitive vocabulary, words can take children only so far. Art picks up where words leave off. The creative process can be a real lifesaver for intuitive children who want to express themselves but can't find the words. It is a chance to express images from deep within, or to share some of the places they "visit" in their intuitive experiences. Even when no one is available to listen, comfort, or share insights, creativity can provide the child with comfort, release, and satisfaction.

ten reasons to support art
with an intuitive child

Creativity is portable, timeless, and something no one can take away. The following are ten reasons why creativity can be especially beneficial for intuitive children:

1. It is fun and helps children reset their inner equilibrium.

2. It is a safe and healthy way to blow off steam and reduce anxiety levels.

3. It moves emotional content at the child's own pace.

4. It is a great way to express big feelings and not be concerned with the impact on other people.

5. It can be combined with most of the ten skills for intuitive kids.

6. It is a safe way to expel an overload of stimuli absorbed during the day.

7. It is a self-esteem boost.

8. It is an open-ended medium for communicating the depths of a child's experience.

9. It is a way to express feelings and still keep the content private.

10. It is a pleasurable multisensory experience.

"but my child isn't into art..."

What if your child isn't into art? Not a problem. Being creative isn't about being an accomplished artist. It is about giving expression, in some authentic way, to what you see, feel, think, and want to communicate. Not every child is drawn to the visual arts for expression. Your child might find a better fit with music, drama, creative writing, poetry, movement, or dance. Or perhaps your child finds a creative zone in the strategy of soccer, making up a new gymnastics routine, or teaching a ball game to friends. You can help children identify their particular expressive form by gently offering a variety of opportunities to explore ways to express themselves. Remind your child that creative expression isn't always about making something beautiful; it is about expressing what is felt inside—also known as "the process." Messes and fun are welcome here.

the bandits that can rob us of a sense of play and creativity

Unrushed pockets of time are the fertile soil for nurturing a deep sense of play, creativity, and contentment. Unstructured time for spontaneous play and creativity allows for an unwinding of stress at the core level. When I think about what kills my playful and creative sprit, I immediately think of stress, too much work, and no free time. In our modern world, we are going against the cultural norm when we carve out real time for play. To do this, we have to be aware of the minefields created by an overly busy, overly structured, task-driven life that can destroy time for meaningful play.

Adults need time for spontaneous play and creativity as well. When we deny ourselves unstructured time to play and unwind, our attitude can spill over onto our children, giving them the message that when they grow up, they will not have time for fun or play. Highly intuitive children will be even more sensitive to these messages. Having fun in family life is great for all children; it can especially benefit a sensitive intuitive child because it resets the day's emotional dial so easily. Since they are so adept at picking up on outside feelings, why not provide a feeling they would be happy to absorb? It is one of the quickest and easiest stress relievers around, unless the bandits of play and creativity are invading your home, as they invade so many homes these days. Here are a few of the bandits that can rob us of a sense of play and creativity in life:

* ★ negativity and judgment about play

* ★ working too much and not allowing for leisure time

* ★ demanding that all time has to be used for important tasks, such as household jobs and work

* ★ seeing art or play as second rate, an extra, or only a treat for when you get all the real work done

★ glorifying the serious adult, puritanical work ethic

★ thinking that it is just something that you do when you're on vacation

★ believing it is only valuable if it produces a good, accomplished product

★ fearing looking silly

★ losing a sense of natural curiosity

If you found yourself identifying with some or all of the bandits, I hope that you won't judge yourself. The items on this list are such an integral part of our modern culture that it's quite challenging not to be impacted by many of these creativity bandits. Keeping in mind that you are benefiting your child's well-being may help to counteract the pull of these bandits.

If you are someone who is challenged in the play area, you might find it helpful to take a look at the following questions and spend some quiet, unhurried time writing down the answers in a journal. It may be helpful to pause for a few minutes before you begin writing, close your eyes, and take a few slow, deep breaths. Allow yourself to relax, let go, and slow down. Breathe. Let all the muscles in your body relax.

Is play of value in my life?

What messages did I receive about being playful as a child?

At what age was I expected to get serious and stop playing so much?

If you played more, what would that look like?

Are you comfortable with your child's playfulness? How about when your child asks you to play? Do you resist or want to dive in?

How does play make your body feel?

Do you have playmates in your adult life? Do they truly accept you?

What kind of play did you enjoy as a child and what is the legacy of play that you would like to offer your child?

What games can you play with your child that will stimulate his creativity and help you to feel closer?

How do you cultivate play in your family life?

What do you need in order to bring more playfulness into your life?

What are your intentions for bringing art, play, and spirit into your home on a regular basis?

How do you think your life would look and feel to you and your family if play were a valued part of every day?

How to Support Creativity in Your Highly Intuitive Child

Dynamic creativity depends on an individual's authentic sense of self-expression. When we feel that we don't have permission to freely express ourselves, then creativity suffers. One of the most important things to be aware of in using art for self-expression is to stay free of a particular goal. This means respecting the process and suspending judgment on the product.

You don't have to be an art therapist to help your intuitive child re-balance via creative expression. Here are some helpful ideas, qualities, and attitudes you should keep in mind as you facilitate your child's creative process:

* ★ Create a safe, nonjudgmental space.
* ★ Give permission to play and explore.
* ★ Have accessible materials and space in the home for creative expression.
* ★ Practice a commitment and belief in the importance of creative time.
* ★ Allow a space for making some messes.
* ★ Find opportunities to say yes to your child when invited into her creative space.

★ Agree on how the art space will be cleaned up so certain family members aren't burdened with the extra work from creative mess making.

★ Allow, allow, allow for the process!

Allowing your child's art to pour forth without analyzing or criticizing it is extremely important. Practice the Zen of letting it be. Maybe your child will want you to be nearby, making some art as well, or maybe your child will want you to just watch while he makes it. Maybe your child will want privacy. As children get to be about 10 or 11 years old, you might notice a change in what they expect of themselves artistically. At about 10 years of age, children often want their art to be representational of reality. Rulers come out in art classes and questions abound of "How do I draw this?" This is the age that most of us stop making expressive art. You can empathize with this wish for things to look realistic and at the same try to come up with other ways to express themselves that don't involve such realistic rendering. I've worked with plenty of children of this age and older who were uncomfortable with their level of mastery over art, and I've had lots of success with them by giving permission for open-ended expression.

Once the art is created it might be tempting to analyze it and ask the child to explain it. I recommend proceeding with care, caution, and respect in discussing children's art. Children can feel violated and unsafe by having an adult judge their art and ask them how they feel or what something means in a picture. Instead, a respectful option can be to just ask an open-ended question like, "Is there anything you want to say about your art?" When children are ready, they will share.

Supporting the Expression of Intense Emotions in Art

Art expression is a wonderful way for intuitive children to get big emotions out onto the paper so they don't stay stuck inside—and result in stress symptoms. Let's take one of the tougher emotions to find safe expression for—anger. When I see anger in art, it often is expressed with a lot of movement. Clay is banged, cut, poked; paper is ripped; oil pastels break under the pressure applied as the person intensely transfers the hot emotion of anger onto the paper. Giving your intuitive child the space to release big feelings like anger through the use of art helps clear out not only other people's anger, which might have been empathically absorbed, but their own anger as well. In general, I find that intuitive children are more inclined toward difficulty with sharing intense emotions like anger because of the high regard they have for relationship harmony and not wanting to upset the people around them. Art can be a safe place for this child to release that hot emotion and experience the power of that release.

In addition to helping your child use art to help resolve these big feelings, you can support her with an open-minded attitude. Staying with the anger example, let your child know that anger is a healthy emotion to feel and she can make safe choices about how to express it. Your child's anger is also an important indicator that a boundary was crossed, and boundaries are an important skill area for intuitive children. Children need to hear that no matter how angry they become, they will still be loved and accepted.

setting the space

Age can drive other factors for artistic expression in the home. What art materials are you willing to have available for a small child? If weather permits, maybe you can designate a space outside as a messy creation zone. If you have space indoors, a corner of a room where you can leave some materials handy for your child can give him a great sense of freedom to act on his impulse to create, without having to go through the negotiation of asking a parent to pull out the art materials. It empowers children to take care of themselves and possibly even self-soothe an upset emotion by easily reaching for handy art media. It also allows you the flexibility to quickly direct your child to the art table when you spot big feelings that could use some immediate attention.

The Spiritual Life of the Highly Intuitive Child

The issue of children's spirituality can be a controversial one, much like the issue of intuition. The term *spirituality* is but one attempt to name the constellation of bigger-than-life experiences that a number of intuitive children experience. As such, the use of the term *spirituality* is associated with the intrinsic, innate experience of the child and not a particular chosen methodology, practice, or religious belief system. As with intuition, it can be quite helpful for children to freely communicate their spiritual experiences with a parent or trusted adult without facing judgment. It bears inclusion in this book because it is an essential ingredient in understanding highly intuitive children. If you are uncomfortable with the term *spirituality*, I invite you to think of this concept in whatever terms work for you.

The spiritual life of many highly intuitive children is often quite rich. Perhaps part of the explanation lies in their big capacity for communicating with realities beyond the traditional five senses. They often push into questions of life and death, creation and destruction on the planet, the origin of one's spirit, the meaning of reincarnation, God, angels, an afterlife, and the list goes on and on. I've known children aged 2 and older who pose these questions frequently and with gusto.

Children who have a gift for spiritual knowing aren't necessarily exposed to it any more than other children, but they can possess a sense of spirituality that comes from deep within. This is different from being religiously precocious. It isn't a knowing that comes from studying text, but rather one that springs from within the child. In the following story, you'll hear about how a child's spirituality plays out with some classic features of intuition and a poignant sense of presence at her grandmother's death.

✳ Mariela — age 4

Poignantly Present with Her Grandmother's Death

Mariela's grandmother was terminally ill, but no one knew this fact. Her grandmother didn't know it, her mother didn't know it, and little Mariela didn't know it at the time. Yet, Mariela spontaneously burst out crying when she would think of her grandmother at random times throughout the year preceding her grandmother's diagnosis with cancer. Perhaps this child's experience wouldn't be quite so surprising if she had been in frequent physical contact with her grandmother, but that wasn't the case. Mariela was living in northern Italy at the time and her grandmother was in a small village in southern Italy, at least a day's travel away. When her mom would check in with her about why she was crying, she said that she was sad about Nonna (Grandma). The tears would always pass quickly, causing no lingering signs of stress for Mariela. Eventually, Nonna's condition became known and her mother was able to identify the cause of her daughter's frequent tears. Mariela's family moved to Nonna's village several months later. Mariela was able to be with her grandmother as her health declined, while still in the safe and loving company of her parents.

One day, as her grandmother was dying in her mom's arms, Mariela made a couple of rainbow pictures with her art materials at Nonna's bedside. Even with barely any writing experience, she quietly wrote "for Nonna" on one of her drawings. During her grandmother's funeral service, a double rainbow could be seen over the church where the services were being held. Mariela's experience at the young age of 4 speaks of both tuning in to the unseen realms of spirituality and her deep empathy that knew no earthly bounds.

Mariela didn't shrink back from the experience of death. Even in the moment of her grandmother's passing, she was at her bedside, making art for her. I find so often that adults fear that death will overwhelm a child, and that they will not be able to fully understand the permanence of death. In her family's loving company, this intuitive child simply followed her truth, experienced the fullness of her gifts, and moved through her grief in her own way.

So how does a parent proceed with supporting the inner spiritual life of a child who comes into the world with this level of perception?

Is it our responsibility to teach them about spirituality, or do we wait for their questions to lead us into the conversation about their development? What parents choose to teach their children about religion and spirituality is deeply personal and influenced by a family's collective history. This can provide a solid grounding place from which their spirits can be nurtured and grow. But highly intuitive, perceptive children can also teach us many things about what it means to be spiritually connected. Children who arrive with a large blueprint for spirituality seem to invite parents into a larger cocreative spiritual life. In the spirit of this cocreation, it may be useful to pay attention to the nature of what your child is asking for with regard to spirituality. Stories can be a wonderful way to help satisfy a child's spiritual hunger. Every spiritual tradition on the planet has stories that we can use to teach children and to help them connect to something bigger in life, and as you'll learn in the following chapter on indigenous wisdom, stories are a centerpiece of this type of teaching.

Highly intuitive children often have a natural understanding of spirituality and sometimes find it hard to feel at home on earth. Sometimes this feeling is expressed as a longing for "home," as in their spirit home. I see this longing as an expression of their ease and comfort in the spiritual realm and the foreignness with which they might experience the earth. In order for highly intuitive children to feel safe in life, they need to feel solidly at home on this planet. If they are bombarded by the problems of today, before they feel the delight and beauty of being alive here, it creates an imbalance within the psyche. So giving them a loving, grounded, stable, accepting place to "land" is extremely important. Children who experience this kind of stress may be especially helped by the grounding skill discussed in Chapter 8.

Lastly, intuitive children may feel even more validated if they have peers who see life through similar eyes. As suggested in Chapter 8, you might find these peers in a children's program or by finding other intuitive kids for your child to spend time with. Parents alone may not fully meet this need. Eventually, children may need the company of others who share their gifts and validate them through experiencing deep, meaningful sharing. If you and your child are having trouble finding like-minded children, having adult friends who are similarly gifted can be a reassurance to the child. In the next chapter focusing on indigenous wisdom, you'll learn more about how the Hawaiian Huna relationship of *hanai* serves this purpose of mentoring in the life of an intuitive child.

what indigenous wisdom can teach us about highly intuitive children

Ambe abinoji aki (Come, child of the earth).

Ojibway friend

Intuitive children often feel alien to the norms of modern culture. This is not true in every culture, and it was not always the case in human history. One of the most fruitful places to look for clues on how to raise an intuitive child is in the teachings of indigenous tribes, cultures, or people. This chapter explores the ancient and current wisdom derived from a few indigenous communities in regard to raising intuitive children and what we can learn from these teachings. We will also explore how the speed of modern-day life could be impacting today's intuitive children.

Indigenous wisdom spans many cultures and is incredibly diverse, but in many wisdom traditions, certain truths emerge time and again. One is the importance of honoring the role of intuition in life. The Ojibway Indian Nation defines intuition with the word *ah-mun'-ni-soo-win*, and one way that the concept is taught is through the story of the Seven Grandfathers. In *The Mishomis Book: The Voice of the Ojibway*, Edward Benton-Banai shares, "After the Clan System was given to the people, the Seven Grandfathers sent seven spiritual beings to earth to clarify how the Clan system was to be used and to amplify the meaning of many gifts often taken for granted in life.... It is said that the first five beings brought messages pertaining to the five senses of man: touch, smell, taste, hearing, and sight. The sixth being brought teachings about ah-mun'-ni-soo-win' (intuition)—a special sense that goes beyond the ordinary senses. It was a special sense that few people recognize in their lives."[1] The Seven Grandfathers' teaching is a good example of how the range of human senses were acknowledged, spoken of, respected, and woven into communal life.

During the course of my research for this book, I spoke with spiritual lineage bearers from the traditions of the Hawaiian Huna (from the lineage of Daddy Bray of Kona, Hawaii), the Eskimo-Inuit from Greenland, and the Maya of Guatemala. In my conversations with these accomplished and wise people who were chosen to practice their healing traditions from a young age, I listened for the clues of how intuitive children were seen, supported, protected, and ultimately, had their gifts, or trait if you will, cultivated. This information comes out of personal interviews I conducted with these remarkable people, and most of this information has been passed down through oral tradition. I am grateful to have been entrusted with these stories so that I may share them with you in the hope that they will empower your parenting.

Indigenous culture is often characterized by a strong emphasis on the value of community. One of the benefits for highly intuitive children growing up within a strongly knit community is that it is not solely up to the parents to recognize and support the gift in their child. If the aunt, uncle, or medicine man were to possess a similar gift, it made it much easier to spot the same in a small child.

Hawaiian Huna: What Can We Learn from this Powerful, Ancient System?

In the ancient Hawaiian culture, the *kahuna* were the shamans, mystics, healers, and spiritual counselors of the village. Although the same cultural structures do not exist today in Hawaii, many of the Huna line-ages continue. In our first cultural visit, I'll take you to Hawaii where I spoke with Dr. Matthew B. James who began his spiritual studies at the young age of 5, under the tutelage of his father, who had studied with Papa Bray in Kona on the island of Hawaii.[2] Dr. James teaches Huna all over the world today, in addition to his work as the president of American Pacific University in Honolulu. He also holds degrees in business and psychology and continues to study with Hawaiian elders and teachers such as Uncle George Naope and Etua Lopes. He was very generous in sharing with me the following insights and teachings of Huna and Hawaiiana that pertain to raising the intuitive children of today around the world.

In ancient Hawaii, the practice of an adult taking on a spiritual mentoring role with a child was sometimes called *hanai* (a form of adoption), which loosely means to be granted a special relationship to an adult who assumes a level of responsibility in the child's personal and spiritual development. This adult was usually someone other than a parent, and the reasons for such a relationship varied depending on the need. For example, there might be a young parent in need of help with raising a child because the parent lacked full emotional maturity, or if a child were recognized as having an intuitive gift that would require special cultivation. When a child was identified by one of the Hawaiian spiritual elders for a hanai relationship, it was because the spiritual essence of the child was seen and recognized. Many of these children displayed gifts of intuitive empathy, but the identifying process was not limited to these traits. Through the hanai relationship, children were offered guidance to cultivate their gifts. In ancient times, the children could be removed from their biological parents to live with their hanai parents, and the children grew up having both biological parents and the hanai parents as guides, teachers, and protectors.

All gifts are held as equal and needed within the Huna community. If a child were born with the gift of healing, visionary insight, and keen intuition, the child could be identified and accepted within the whole of the tribe. One of the beautiful aspects of this system was that these children also had someone to go to who understood what it felt like to have these abilities and could offer them the specific training and developmental guidance that they needed to mature with balance. They were not alone. Today's intuitive children (and their parents) can often feel ostracized and, because of this, experience undue stress; the Huna system of inclusion and respect for differences minimizes this kind of stress.

The Huna tradition values intuitive gifts in children and conveys messages to their children of valuing these gifts. They don't elevate or denigrate the gift, but rather, meet it in a respectful and purposeful manner. Children can know that their gifts are valued when the adults around them appreciate the perspective and insights they bring.

Since the Hawaiian culture took these gifts seriously, it was poised to offer specific kinds of parenting and training for children exhibiting these gifts. The *kahuna* and *kupuna* (elders) knew that children with these traits had some special capabilities and with them came certain social and cultural expectations. For example, highly intuitive children were taught that it is impolite to "read" someone intuitively and then simply walk up to the person and announce their findings.

Now when a child innocently crosses a boundary like this one, the child might be told not to ever do that again. Children can interpret a "rule" like this to mean they should not use their intuition. Although it is understandable for parents to want to set a boundary on a child's intuitive intrusion, they also need to know it is a learning process. We can learn from the Huna that when we receive intuitive messages, we can practice the finer nuances of how to communicate these appropriately, with respect and humility.

Intuitive children can benefit from lessons on intuitive manners. With intuitive manners, the child learns how to act with respect for others in regard to their abilities. One example is learning that it is inappropriate to walk up to a stranger and deliver an intuitive message about the person. Just as we wouldn't expect a small child to automatically know our expectations about table manners, it is unfair to expect that they would automatically know intuitive manners as well. Small children routinely eat with their mouths open, and young intuitive kids might walk up to strangers and provide their insights or even ask very direct, innocent, intuitive questions. This is quite natural until they understand more appropriate social behavior. Of course, manners vary based on family and cultural values, so it is up to each family to determine appropriateness while, at the same time, supporting their child's intuition.

Intuitive children growing up in the Hawaiian community were able to take their time to grow, develop, and just be "kids." They were offered plenty of time to grow in their self-esteem and plant their intuitive knowledge firmly in their physical body, creating a sense of harmony in life. They learned the meaning of the Hawaiian value of patient perseverance through the living example of the adults around them. And the adults responsible for their development astutely timed lessons that were appropriate, depending on the mental, emotional, and intuitive readiness of the child.

Being seen, witnessed, valued, respected, supported, and held to certain levels of responsibility contributed to mastery of the gift, or trait, within the child. Children were never expected to accomplish these tasks on their own, for they had the support of the community and especially someone who had walked a path with similar gifts before them. With the guidance of someone who knew the unique life challenges and joys of this gift, children were able to accomplish the task of being firmly and happily rooted here on earth, while fully expressing their intuitive gifts.

We can't go back to ancient times and the communal structure that existed long ago, but we can incorporate some of these insightful practices into modern parenting. The hanai relationship of the Huna speaks to the concept that seeing gifts in our children need not be solely the job of the parent. If my child were born a musical virtuoso, I would be out of luck in providing her training in her instrument to the degree of her ability. But I could value the gift and find someone to support and nourish it in developmentally appropriate ways. Likewise, it might be possible to find other adults who can help cultivate the gift of intuitive empathy and know how to offer your family pertinent support. Perhaps you and your child can find support with a relative, a friend, teacher, or therapist. Indigenous wisdom is proof that it takes a village to raise a child—in fact, it quite literally did.

Inuit Wisdom and Intuitive Children

Our next stop on the journey of indigenous wisdom and the highly intuitive child takes us to Greenland, known as Kalaallit Nunaat by the Inuit natives there, and home to the Eskimo-Inuit shaman, Angaangaq.[3] Angaangaq, who is also known as Uncle to his people and around the world, is a very busy shaman. He is on an extremely important mission because the great ice sheet covering his homeland is melting rapidly. The importance of his message has taken him to five continents and more than forty countries around the world, and he has met with various world leaders, including Nelson Mandela and the Dalai Lama.

Angaangaq exudes a warmth and wisdom that comes through in all of his words. He is sincere, kind, and truly cares about the next generation. As we talked about intuition and the next generation, he pondered out loud about the challenges of passing on the old ways and teachings to the next generation. Angaangaq was fortunate to have grown up with the old ways through the teachings of his grandmothers and other elders. Raised in the ways of a shaman and teacher, he told me during our interview, "Intuition is the only way the tribe operates. The older generation told us how to be with it, how to trust it. It's what keeps us all going." He also teaches that intuition is capable of "helping us touch other realities and be better aware of ourselves…and then we can live in a good way." Angaangaq's grandmothers taught him that intuitive feelings are the most important and that he had to learn how to live with them. They also helped to pass along a respect for intuitive wisdom. He stated, "It is what keeps the society and people strong. It is what allows it [life] to be."

Today, Angaangaq credits his intuition and the wisdom that has been passed down through his elders as the foundation for his way of seeing life. He tries hard to live his grandmothers' teachings and admits, "It is easier to talk about it than to live it."

Angaangaq finds himself in an agonizing struggle today because he is living "between worlds." Because of the impact of modern life, consumerism, and global warming, the world that he grew up in is no longer, and today's Eskimo-Kalaallit are struggling with a very difficult way of life. Angaangaq said that because the world is changing, his culture has changed, and therefore the old ways that have always supported children in understanding the interweaving of intuition and physical life are disappearing. As he spoke, I could feel and hear the pain in his voice. Clearly, this is an elder who cares profoundly for the next generation—and for the planet. His voice lifted as I asked him if the little children seek him out. "Oh, yes! They come to me for the stories. Without stories we have nowhere to go." I smiled, thinking of small children gathering at Uncle's feet to hear his stories or hear him play his medicine drum.

I asked if he sees the children dreaming a new, beautiful dream for the planet, to which he said with utmost clarity in his voice, "I am confident that the children are dreaming a new world." Finally, I asked him if he has any message for the children. He gave this message from his heart:

> *All hope is not gone*
> *There is so much hope worth having today*
> *The world is an incredibly beautiful place*
> *And it is worth having*
> *We need to have an incredible embracing of the world*
> *We can't afford not to embrace the world in which we live.*
>
> — Angaangaq, 2008

Angaangaq ended this teaching about the children by sharing that it is our responsibility to give all children this dream. When he told me this, I felt his words deep in my heart, fanning the embers of love and passionate commitment in a way that only wise words can. We parted with his reminder, "We are all responsible for the return of joy to our hearts."

Children around the world need to remember this dream, and our sensitive, empathic children who feel the pain of the world need to have this dream of hope well anchored in their psyches. Angaangaq is an intuitive who lives this message, and I think it is a very important one for today's intuitive children.

The Maya Voice of Wisdom

Guatemalan Maya Elder Mercedes B. Longfellow shared her culture's wisdom for intuitive children with me.[4] Mercedes is a Maya Mam Aj'q'ij' (ahk qik) from the highlands of Guatemala. The Aj'q'ij' is the Maya lineage carrier and highest spiritual guide within the community. Mercedes grew up amid the traditions that you will read about next, and later moved to the United States where she continues to teach Maya wisdom both here and around the world. Mercedes began our interview by sharing, "The children of light are being born and are very wise." Mercedes is not singling out highly intuitive children as the special, wise ones. In fact, she conveys a cautionary note about viewing any child's gifts as better than another's: "All children are beautiful." The love and respect she feels for children was palpable.

To understand the Maya view on intuition in children, we need to view it within the context of the community. Although some children are observed to have a stronger aptitude for intuition and clear perception in life, this is not seen as a singular gift, but rather a tool. The tool is part of the tool kit that the child will need to complete his mission in life. For example, if the child's mission is to teach others the delicate knowledge of the universe, the child might draw on intuition, depending on what is needed in the mission.

The concept of a person's mission, or life purpose, is fundamental to how parents raise their children within the Maya community. According to Mercedes, when a baby is born, the parents visit the highest spiritual guide within the community—the Aj'q'ij'. The visit with the Aj'q'ij' provides the parents of the newly born baby with information about the child's life purpose, based on the Maya cosmology, one detail of which has to do with the meaning of the day the child was born. The Aj'q'ij' shares a clear picture with the parents about the child's mission, and this highly regarded information becomes the basis for tailoring parenting specifically to this child. Because of this precisely attuned parenting, informed by life purpose, no two children are treated the same way, and parents act with confidence and peaceful hearts in their parenting.

Families are in a constant relationship with the Aj'q'ij' within the community. If the child and parents were to have difficulty in the years to come, they could seek out the help of the Aj'q'ij' as needed. But, as Mercedes shares, this help is rarely needed because the children and families live in deep harmony. How is it that these people experience such inner and outer harmony?

Part of the answer lies in the connection that individuals have, from birth, to their purpose or mission. Mercedes shares that everything begins with the parents when it comes to raising a child. Parents pay great attention to making sure that they are prepared for this work by knowing themselves first.

The loving empathy and respect that they hold for their child, coupled with their own personal knowing, helps to ensure the success of the most important parenting task: bringing out the child's organic wisdom. It is clear to Mercedes that when the child is raised with love, patience, and understanding, the child can express his or her wisdom more readily than children who do not receive this kind of parenting. Respectful parenting creates the environment for the child, and the environment shapes the unfolding of gifts and wisdom.

Another aspect of this harmony is created through the social fabric of the community. The Maya share laws in common that guide behavior, also known as *medicine*. One of these medicine laws is that of respect. The teachings about respect guide the Maya child to leave things as they are, that everything has a place on this earth, everything has a place in our lives, and to not take possession of life. Respect is extended to all life forms, and we are not to disrupt the fine balance of life. If we do, the lack of balance transfers into our relationships and families.

Evidence of putting this medicine into practice is found in the ritual of daily talking circles in the community. Each day, time is taken for gathering together to talk about problems and needs and to work to make things right among the people. "Psychologists are not needed," Mercedes pointed out, "thanks to our circles." This is a tradition dating back to ancient times and she feels that this kind of balance is part of what is missing in our society today.

As I think of sensitive, empathic, intuitive children growing up in the closely knit Maya community, I sense the ease and support for them. Their gifts are seen, acknowledged, and held with respect—in equal measure to everyone else's gifts and mission. Empathic children feel the safety created by living within a family that respects one from the start and that practices a daily commitment to clear communication. Parents, community, and the Aj'q'ij' all stand by the child's side, ready to help if needed. I can tell that many of the stressors discussed in this book are largely absent for highly intuitive children in the Maya community, due to the finely attuned support received on all levels.

The traditional Maya model of community and child rearing speaks of a wisdom largely missing from our modernized world. In the absence of having an Aj'q'ij' to turn to, what can we receive from these teachings? We can remember that parenting that comes from the heart truly does matter. Creating time to stay balanced within ourselves matters. Establishing regular times to maintain harmony with each other matters. Keeping in mind our relationship with all of life, and that our children are born with an inherent wisdom that we can listen for, cultivate, and celebrate, matters deeply. Mercedes reminds us that our children need to feel at home here and they need us to help them express their own wisdom. She closed our interview with a special message: "May we treat the children with our tender loving care for the future of the planet."

Intuitive Time vs. Linear Time and the Impact on Intuitive Children

According to Angaangaq, all time is intuitive time from the perspective of the old ways of his tribe. So the notion of evaluating the difference between intuitive and linear time is a Western construct. What does it mean to be in intuitive time rather than in linear time? Linear time is ruled by the clock. It goes in only one forward direction and is scheduled and regulated based on a set of points in time. If you plan a point in time and miss it, there's no going back. Busy, stressful schedules and constantly having to think about the future is a product of linear time. Obviously we have to plan for things in life, but when we are caught too much in linear time, we get locked into thinking constantly about the future, feeling squeezed, stressed, and pushed. By contrast, intuitive time is informed by the great, slower rhythms and cycles of life—the sun, moon, and stars traversing across the sky, the seasons and their teachings about life, the eternal return of day and night.

In intuitive time, we have space to listen to our own inner guidance. There is room to respond to the questions, "What do I want to do next?" "Is this safe for me?" "Is this of my highest good?" "How is my body feeling about this?" It isn't rushed, pushed, or demanding. Intuitive children can benefit from regular juicy pauses of time that allow them the freedom to explore as they wish. A good book, some art, daydreaming, time in nature, and even playing with friends can all do the trick of helping them realign with this slower rhythm within.

how the linear time push can impact an intuitive student

Children can't always be in charge of taking these juicy pauses in the day and taking care of personal needs. The following example describes how a teacher's style can impact an intuitive student in the classroom.

✳ **Sherry — age 10**

An Intuitive Child Struggling in a Fast-Paced Sensate Classroom

Sherry, a highly intuitive child in a fast-paced public-school classroom, reported that highly structured, fact-pushing assignments, "make me feel tight, sickish, and give me a headache. I want to zone out because I can't take any more of it, but then I'm embarrassed if the teacher calls on me and I wasn't paying attention. I just can't take it anymore, though." Sherry described a preference for open-ended discovery where she could work more at her own pace, with or without a team of other students. She found this style of learning fun and her body felt great when she was engaged in a learning style that was a good fit for her needs.

Sherry experienced a full year with a teacher who held to a quick-paced, detail-packed curriculum with little room for open-ended discovery. She experienced higher stress that year that needed consistent rebalancing at home. Sherry also had a teacher later who valued open-ended discovery, moved at a slower pace, and practiced frequent pauses for fun. Her stress was much lower that year, with her parents needing to focus much less on stress reduction.

Sherry's story points to issues of needing a good fit between student and teacher and also speaks to what can happen when an intuitive student is excessively rushed in the classroom, or elsewhere.

intuitive leaps of time and understanding

For a highly intuitive person, intuitive time is not always experienced as slow and calm. Intuitive flashes often arrive at great speed in an acceleration of understanding. Suddenly, an intuitive will have the solution to a problem but have no idea how she arrived at the end result. So, in a certain sense, intuitive insights can bypass the bounds of linear time with great speed. However, it doesn't feel rushed. It is more like a quickening, or a leap. This is a different experience than feeling rushed, hurried, and stressed in linear time, and constantly thinking about the future. Intuitive knowing about people, places, animals, and even world events can come at an astonishingly rapid speed. Sometimes intuitive leaps, including predictions, will frighten children who suddenly can intuitively see things for which they don't have a context. When this happens, it can outpace a child's emotional development. Whether it is experienced as an acceleration of personal understanding or getting a read on something related to other people or even the planet, the child might feel scared and overwhelmed with the knowledge. Adults can support children in these experiences by listening attentively, reminding the child that there is nothing wrong with having these kinds of insights, and offering comfort if the child is upset by what she sees.

troubleshooting problems with time navigation in parenting

Regardless of whether or not your child is intuitive, modern family life is packed with many negotiations about how to spend each day and maneuver within a time frame. This is even more of an issue for a child who is highly intuitive. Take, for example, the challenge of a child who is normally pretty comfortable in his morning routine, but who on this particular morning is desperate for some of that intuitive time that isn't ruled by the clock. It is 8:00 AM and it is time to leave for school and work. Your child is dreamily playing with the dog, his hair and teeth are not brushed, and he could not care less about needing to leave or being late. It can be tough when these two realities of time converge on each other. So what do you do? Well, when it isn't negotiable, it is possible to practice limit setting and reflective listening while, for example, combing your child's hair. Here's how this one would look: "I can see/-hear how much you would love to play more with the dog right now, and I wish we had time for that. If we did that right now, though, you'd be late for school. Let's make sure that you get more time with Sparky after school." Underneath this conversation, you can use your own intuition and investigate why this is so important to your child. Did the child have a bad dream and is in need of extra comfort? Is there something the child is worried about in school, or does the child need more play? For young children, when you acknowledge their needs, set a limit, and negotiate an alternative, you may find your child feeling more clearly heard and maybe even behaving more flexibly.

If your child is having sudden resistance to your routine at home, it might be time to rethink the rhythm of the rest of the day. Is your child working hard at school and participating in a lot of extracurricular activities, with little downtime when away from home? Is your child acting out, unusually irritable, or easily frustrated? Is this a call for help in finding more time to rebalance or to build in more flexibility in the child's life? Another thing to watch out for is the possibility of your child tuning out because she isn't getting enough downtime. Children are creative and resilient. They'll get their needs met one way or another, and if they aren't getting enough time to relax and decompress, they might take that downtime right in the middle of their least favorite subject in school.

A common problem is the overscheduled child. It takes a conscious choice not to overschedule most children. Some children thrive on a packed schedule, and you may have an intuitive child who can keep up with a rigorous schedule. But many intuitives seem to do better with some breathing room in their days. This downtime can help them let go of the emotional dynamics and conflicts that they may absorb throughout the day. It also provides a break from overstimulation in general. If you are wondering if your child's current schedule is a help or hindrance, take a moment to ask or observe whether the activities help rebalance the child or add to stress levels.

art suggestions for helping children who struggle with time

The following are some suggestions to implement and some questions you can ask your child:

⋆ Have the child draw a picture of the tension he feels when being rushed. Ask the child, "What does it feel like in your body?" "If you could draw a picture of the inside of your head, what would be in there?" "How does it make your tummy feel?"

⭑ Allow the child to show you how it feels by acting it out with stuffed animals or toys.

⭑ Give plenty of space, creative arts materials, and time for the inner tensions to be expressed and for the transformational essence to be released in the psyche. Remember, we don't have to make this happen; we get to facilitate and witness the unfolding of this process.

⭑ Children who are feeling pressured by always having to be somewhere at an appointed time might like to do some art on an inexpensive teaching clock that can be found in teaching supply stores. Ideas include drawing a new system for keeping time on the clock and changing the time on the clock any way that the child would like.

all grown up now

One must still have chaos in oneself
to be able to give birth to a dancing star.

FRIEDRICH WILHELM NIETZSCHE

The long-term effects of being raised in a family that can't see, let alone empathize with, one's gifts can be troubling and can create wounds that can last long into adulthood unless addressed. Adults who were told as children that their intuitions about others were weird, crazy, or impolite run the risk of burying their connection to their inner truth. I know it is possible to reclaim the power of intuitive empathy in adulthood because I have witnessed these transformations firsthand. In therapy, I help these adults unpack old, faulty beliefs about themselves that have grown into false layers of their identity. As they recover the freedom to contact their intuitive truth, life takes on a rich aliveness. Hearing inner guidance is easier, decision making is clearer, personal dreams resurface, interpersonal boundaries transform, and creativity flows happily again.

I can spot an intuitive empath pretty quickly, probably because I am one and have personally lived the challenges and gifts of these traits. When I start to ask highly intuitive clients the questions that help to identify an intuitive empath (like the questions in Chapter 1), a common ground develops as we define the blessings and challenges of being highly intuitive. Usually I see palpable relief on people's faces when their intuitive gifts are recognized: "You mean I'm not crazy?" "I'm not weird?" "I'm not too sensitive?" I inform these people that there are, in fact, many kindred spirits with their abilities—people who speak their language and who also may know the need to take care of sensitive bodies and energy levels in ways that may seem odd and even indulgent to others.

What Intuitive Adults Can Teach Us about Parenting Intuitive Children

My reasons for including the stories of intuitive adults in this book are multifaceted. First of all, it is important to recognize the role that parents and other key adults play in an intuitive child's life. Positive attitudes and skillful help will make a big difference in your child's success. In the following stories you will read about two women. One received the parental support that I advocate in this book and one did not. By including the perspective of adult intuitives, you get to take a preview peek at what might lie ahead in the years to come and think about the kind of support you want your child to have now. If we can spot the intuitive child and attend to the child's unique needs now, then the need to reparent and excavate the true self later in life can be avoided.

✳ Dana — age 38

Healing as an Adult Intuitive

Dana's parents were accomplished scientists at the top of their games. Her father was a surgeon and her mother a research scientist in oncology at a prestigious Ivy League university. Dana had two older brothers and came from a long line of MDs and PhDs. Dana was smart, savvy, and accomplished in her own right as a professor in international economics. Her family was thrilled with her recent accomplishment of being selected as the head of the department at her university, but she felt miserable. That was when Dana decided to call me.

Dana arrived at my office for her first visit and settled in on the couch with a look of trepidation. She had already shared with me on the phone that her old, familiar discontent was settling in again, this time spurred by high stress and professional dissatisfaction during her late thirties. As Dana started to tell me her story now in person, I noticed how carefully she was looking for some kind of judgment on my face. I checked in to see how she was doing this far in our session. She gathered her courage to determine how I felt talking about intuition and I shared my openness. Her body relaxed. My body relaxed. She began to tell her story about feeling judged and only partially seen by her former therapists who didn't quite understand the extent of her intuition and its impact on her life.

As the session progressed, the dance of question-and-answer between us flowed and started to open a door that she had forgotten existed. Behind that door were the rich stories of how she was known for being a child empathetic to other children, babies, and pets. She was the one who could tell why the cat was acting strange, why the baby continued to cry after being fed and changed, and why the toddler wouldn't settle down. Because of the negative messages she received as a child about her intuition, her abilities were buried, but not completely forgotten. As I spoke of some of the ideas presented in this book, she began to realize that she had found a therapist who understood her abilities, and letting out a deep sigh, she said, "Thank you. I've always felt judged and misunderstood for these abilities. Maybe there is hope to see this as a gift."

Dana explained that she felt an aching absence of meaning in her life. The ladder she'd climbed to her success had been steep and precarious and she was no stranger to stress on an ongoing basis. She was exhausted from the relentless demands of the job and her own perfectionism. "You know I wouldn't have minded all the hard work," she explained, "if only it was for something that I felt passionate about, but the truth is that I feel like I'm a guest in the show of my own life. I'm tired of saying someone else's lines." More than anything in the world, Dana dreamed of starting a nonprofit company in support of inner city children and having more time to spend in her garden the way she had as a child. She was hungry to take classes to develop her intuition but she was scared of tuning in to this part of herself that had caused her so much grief as a child. I thought this held a clue and wanted to know more.

As a child, Dana loved going into the garden because it was where she felt peaceful and her mind could go quiet. She pointed out that her garden time felt like her recent explorations of meditation, which she was studying for stress management. When she hung out in her own personal garden plot of flowers, she often would have thoughts and impressions that would pass through her mind about people she knew, and she explained that later she came to realize that there was no way she could have known these things rationally. One day, 5-year-old Dana had an image float up in her mind about her teacher being sick and she thought, "My teacher needs to go to the doctor to find out what's wrong." She wasn't scared, but it stood out as something that she simply needed to do. The next day after school, Dana innocently walked up to her kindergarten teacher, who happened to be on yard duty, and shared her thought. Her teacher was immediately shocked because unbeknownst to her little student, she'd been to her ob-gyn the day before to have a lump checked out for cancer. Her teacher caught her breath, smiled, and thanked Dana for being so thoughtful. That was the moment Dana's mom came running onto the scene.

What Dana hadn't realized was that her mom was actually within earshot on the playground, ready to take her home from school. When Dana's mom overheard her giving this warning, she flushed red with embarrassment and immediately ran over to stop the exchange. She apologized to the teacher, who assured her that no apology was needed, and she then hurriedly scooted Dana off to a private spot on the playground. She told Dana in no uncertain terms that she was never, ever, to do something like that again. Dana didn't quite understand what her mom was talking about, but she did realize that she had better be quiet about those kinds of ideas— even with her mom.

That day informed much of the rest of Dana's life up until this point. Dana routinely squelched her intuitive messages and internally criticized herself for having them in the first place. The constant denial of her inner messages was taking a high toll on her ability to trust herself. Instead, she turned to taking care of others.

Dana liked to experience harmony with others because it made her feel better, if only temporarily, to make other people happy. Even if it came at the expense of not listening to her own personal needs. Now, she found that she was taking care of so many other people that it was hard to even hear her own inner truth. One thing was crystal clear to Dana, however; intuitive insights were taboo and she was wrong for having them. In the space of that vacuum created by suppressing her own inner knowing, she filled up her life with overwork, doing things to please other people, and chasing her parents' dream for her life. At nearly 40 years of age, she was tired of this false life. Like so many truths that can bubble to the surface, she knew that what was happening had to stop but she didn't have a clear vision yet of what she wanted to create for herself.

Dana had spent years living the life that she thought would please other people. First, it was her parents and teachers and then it became her employer, a prestigious university. Especially now, it was taking increasing amounts of energy to keep up with the endless demands of that new position. Teetering on exhaustion, she could see that it was time to do something different, something personally meaningful, but she was scared. We started our work with creating a sense of safety. Dana had not grown up in what we would consider an unsafe environment. Her parents loved her, fed her, didn't hurt her, and wanted the best for her. She just had one major need missing: that of being seen and appreciated for who she was with a trait that was fundamental to her personality and experience of life.

Dana was the round peg trying to fit into the square hole. She was an intuitive feeler type on the Myers-Briggs scale, and she could relate to having at one time the turbocharge on her intuitive feeler abilities until they grew dormant over time. The people in her family, on the other hand, were sensate thinker types on the Myers-Briggs scale who could not relate to the subtle world of intuitive empathy. Dana was pegged from an early age as the one in the family who was too sensitive, melodramatic, and had those crazy visions about other people's troubles. She was acutely aware of feeling different in her family, at school, and in the world at large. Capable of reading people's emotions and needs from a very young age, she concluded that it was in her best survival interests to try to fit into the norm and put a lid on this other side of herself.

When we try to put a lid on a defining trait that is integral to our life force, we are asking for trouble. Although it makes good sense to know when, how, and who to reveal intuitive, empathic information to in life, a full-out suppression is a drastic response. Children might not have much of a choice in the matter and decide that it is better to hide this part of themselves in order to gain the love and acceptance of their peers and parents. What is often forgotten, however, is that what once was a smart survival tactic as a child, can evolve into an ingrained belief about oneself. Part of the work with recovering intuitives is helping them to see that it is safe to be themselves—perhaps for the first time.

Dana's outer life as a successful professor stood as an example of someone who could apply a great deal of inner discipline in staying in a line of work that was not her dream job. Dana was very intelligent, so she could master the complex information that came with her subject matter and she could often leap to understandings on theories that left her colleagues wondering how she could just "get" certain complexities so easily. This ability to leap out to an intuitive conclusion and then have to work backward to fill in the details of how she arrived there is a classic feature of the intuitive type in the Jungian framework. From that perspective, Dana was fairly comfortable working with her own nature.

The place that she was having more trouble with lay in what I call the "energetics" of being an intuitive type. She was suppressing her intuitive, instinctive knowing and paying a high price for having this guidance go silent inside. For one thing, this disconnect was getting very confusing for her. Her heart and her gut would say one thing, and she would routinely override the message with her head. The chronic override of her internal wisdom had caused her to go soft in her ability to hear her instinctive knowing. She had lost her ability to know truth in her body as she once had as a child. Now her body seemed to scream at her with various aches and pains (especially when she was overdoing for others), but it was hard to get at the subtleties of a clear yes or no when tuning in to her inner guidance. Perhaps the biggest problem overall for Dana was that she was struggling over self-trust in so many areas of her life. She was not trusting her body wisdom and lacked the trust to leave the conjured safety of success and change jobs to something that was more meaningful for her. Could she do it?

Dana did do it. First, we excavated the messages that no longer fit for her. One of these messages was about the power that she continued to give her mother when she forbid her to speak of her intuitions and what it had cost her to dedicate her life to the rational at the expense of a balance between both. She vowed to take that power back and speak her truth when possible. In therapy she had ample opportunity to speak all of her truths and to be witnessed by someone who wouldn't judge her. Through this process, her deepest truths surfaced—just waiting to be shared. Oftentimes a highly intuitive adult can wait a lifetime for this experience. When someone realizes there is nothing wrong with the way they perceive life, even if it is different from the dominant culture, it lifts a huge weight off the person. This is energy that can then be applied to jettisoning outdated behaviors and living life with purpose, passion, and joy.

Discarding Outdated Coping Skills

Dana's work wasn't complete simply by realizing that her intuition was a gift and not a curse. Now she faced the work of honestly looking at all the ways she had created a life for others and denied herself the riches of her own heart's desires. Taking excessive care of others was a major drain on her body, her emotions, and her ability to be close with people.

At an early age, Dana stumbled on the realization that if she could cheer up others, she somehow started to feel better. Her motivation didn't necessarily come from generosity (although she is exceedingly kind). It started out as that classic "Your stress is my stress" phenome-non. When one of her family members felt lousy, she could feel the sen-sations in her own body. Maybe it was a stomachache, or a headache, or just a sense of tension and unease. When she realized that if she cheered up the family member and made the person's stress vanish, she would feel better too, she thought she'd found the key to her happiness. Long-ing to feel better, Dana decided to do this routinely in her life. She never quite realized that she was often trying to not feel other people's feelings so strongly. No one ever even knew she was doing this; it all flew under the radar of her family, who did not share this trait. Understandably, her parents just figured Dana had a knack for cheering up other people. And she sure did—but at a cost.

Dana jettisoned this behavior by first understanding the how and why behind creating it in the first place. Like so many childhood behav-iors, it once served her on some level but was costing her dearly now. In therapy Dana learned to observe other people's moods, pains, and disappointments and to stay in her own experience. When she took on other people's moods, vibrating to them like a tuning fork, she learned that she could let go of those using some of the skills presented in Chap-ter 8. When she stayed with the subtle cues of her own body, she found that it provided her a great deal of data. This data was only clear so long as she took great care of herself and could tell the difference between what was her own feeling and what belonged to someone else. It took many trial-and-error experiences of walking into rooms feeling okay, and then leaving the room feeling someone else's lousy mood or ache or pain, to see that she could practice some choice in these situations. Dana worked hard on grounding, on pulling in her antenna, on cultivating her own knowledge of yes and no signals in her body, on creating a new ap-preciation of her right to set boundaries, and on truly trusting herself. Her self-trust grew with each success in practicing these new skills and awareness.

As her therapy continued, Dana began to discover the joy of being authentic, and she found her appreciation for her life growing by leaps and bounds. Before making peace with her intuitive, empathic nature, Dana seemed a bit adrift and never quite connected to her own ability to define her life to her specifications. It was always life on someone else's terms. All of that was changing now. Dana finally felt the thrill and possibility of creating the life of her dreams.

With the extra energy and spring in her step as a result of not over-giving in relationships, she now had some extra motivation to put her nonprofit dream into action. Her intuition guided her to the right people to speak with and to other favorable conditions for a start-up. Her keen people skills were her ally, and because she was working on something so aligned with her own dream, she found herself springing into action with an aliveness that she hadn't felt since she was a child in the garden. In her spare time, she kept a dream journal and spent time with other new friends who shared some of her abilities. Dana had come home to herself.

✳ Angie — age 46

Growing Up with Strong Support

Angie grew up in what I would consider near ideal circumstances for a highly intuitive child, and she has grown to be a woman confident and at peace with the trait. Now in her forties, she is the principal of an alternative high school that serves a diverse group of teens. Angie is known for being a fair, kind, and downright charismatic leader to both the students and faculty. She explains, "Teens these days need someone who can see them at their level. It's easy for me to slip into their experience and feel what they are going through. I also have a pretty good sense for when they are lying to me or need extra help but are unwilling to ask for it," Her seamless weaving of her intuitive empathy on the job gives her an advantage of being especially successful in most of her relationships across the board. It is second nature to Angie.

Occasionally, she grows tired of all of the teen and bureaucratic drama involved with running a high school, and she can reach a tipping point of feeling burdened, especially if her schedule squeezes her to the point of not being able to eat well and practice yoga daily. When she dips into high stress, she is particularly vulnerable to picking up on other people's negativity and even feeling the deeper pain of the world. When she feels such negativity, she quickly pays attention and increases her level of self-care to regain balance.

What is the secret to Angie's success with the trait, and why did she not need to recover her gift later in life? The answer to this lies largely in the parenting she received as a child. Angie was fortunate to have one highly intuitive parent who instinctively knew that she wanted to keep her daughter's intuition alive as a child. Her mother had not been so lucky and had spent a lot of time as an adult reclaiming the trait largely on her own through reading, taking classes, and listening to her intuition. Angie's father was a sensate-thinker type who didn't relate completely with his daughter's trait, but he never expressed judgment or the expectation that she should try to be anyone other than her true self. Angie shined in this balanced parenting. She knew she could bring her more unusual intuitive experiences to her mom and have them immediately validated, but she wouldn't hesitate to share them with her father if she wanted to.

Angie knew that both of her parents loved her and accepted her to the core. They also trusted that she was growing at just her own pace, learning what she needed as she grew. Her parents' trust and acceptance held her like terra firma. Angie was also fortunate to have a mother who instinctively taught her some versions of the skills that you've learned in this book. One of the especially interesting gifts that her mother gave her was teaching her how to meditate. Angie still meditates on a regular basis as an adult and has found that her meditation practice is key to shaking off other people's stress that she occasionally takes on. Meditation also helps to keep her own positive energy high and her stress levels low.

I attribute a large part of Angie's great success to her strong sense of self-esteem. Her strong connection to her inner truth and her own needs, wants, and dreams keep her naturally grounded in her own experience. Although she struggled to some degree with the challenges found in this book, she also had the benefit of forty years to keep building and developing skills in her own time and in a way that worked uniquely for her. Angie didn't need to recover her intuitive empathy because it was never forced underground. Part of the hope of this book is to support more families in keeping this trait alive in their children so that they can thrive with it throughout life like Angie continues to do.

Are You an Adult Intuitive Recovering Your Intuitive Gifts?

If you can relate to the experience of needing to reclaim your intuitive strengths, take heart; it is possible to come back home to yourself and make peace with this aspect of your nature. The challenges that adults experience with this trait can be similar to those faced by children, with some obvious differences as well. One of the most striking differences has to do with simply living more years with the challenging aspects of this trait and the chronic stressors that can emerge over time.

taking inventory: common challenges of highly intuitive and empathic adults before integration

As the following list demonstrates, these stressors can translate into uncomfortable behaviors and beliefs that get in the way of living an authentic life.

- ⋆ frequently overgiving in relationships to try to fix, make peace, create, or restore a sense of harmony

- ⋆ confusion about boundaries, both interpersonally and energetically

- ⋆ inexplicable aches, pains, and body sensations around different people

- ⋆ elevating other people's needs above your own to the detriment of being able to hear and act on your own needs

- ⋆ foggy sense of self-trust, since the core of self-trust has been buried

- ⋆ existential guilt, fatigue, or being overwhelmed by being privy to intuitive data and warnings about people and events without knowing what to do with this information

★ hungry to be seen and acknowledged at a deep level by people who can relate with your perceptions in life

★ existential stress that manifests as feeling uncomfortable with human existence and drawing increasingly from spiritual sustenance for meaning and support, which translates into feeling "more at home in spirit than on earth"

★ wanting to fit in more or toughen up in order to be more like other people

★ waning energy due to suppressing intuitive empathy, and consequently, suppressing one's spirit; over time, feeling tired trying to wear a "mask" to fit into the dominant culture

★ a tendency toward perfectionism as a means of making the external world more organized and as a perceived means of calming down anxiety

★ engaging in addictive behavior in order to drown out the excessive noise and stress often associated with intuitive overload

How This Is Different from Codependency

Often when I describe the common characteristics of adults recovering their intuitive trait, I'll hear "Yes, but that's just like codependency." Yes and no; allow me to clarify. The characteristics on the list that relate to a hyperfocus on other people can easily be misconstrued as codependency. Clearly, it is possible to be both highly codependent and highly intuitive. However, intuitively absorbing someone else's negative emotions is not the same as codependency. Codependency is characterized by focusing more on other people's needs at the expense of your own and is driven by the need to be needed by other people, which defines a codependent's self-worth. For intuitive empaths, the excessive focusing on the needs of others is often driven by the tendency to absorb someone else's negative emotions and then trying to find a way to feel better. This can result in a desire to make the other person feel better so that the highly intuitive person doesn't have to continue absorbing and vibrating with the uncomfortable feelings in their body. In other words, whereas the codependent is often driven by a need to get something (feeling needed and worthy), the highly intuitive person is often driven by a need to get rid of something (someone else's negative emotions).

Adults reclaiming intuitive empathy are not codependents. In my experience, intuitive adult clients who mastered the suggestions in this book experienced a decline in behaviors that mimic codependency.

Embracing Your Feelings in the Healing Process

The road to reclaiming intuitive empathy in an adult's life when it has been derailed for any reason can bring up a wide range of feelings and is a distinctively personal journey. I've spoken of the relief that washes over many adults when they finally hear about this trait and connect their life experiences to what is typically felt by other intuitives. The knowledge that we aren't alone is very comforting and empowering.

The healing doesn't stop there. Grief can be a likely next step in the healing process. Imagine carrying around a heavy backpack laden with beliefs about yourself that there is something about you that is strange, abnormal, and painfully different. If I told you, "You were never meant to carry that pack. It is filled with faulty belief systems," I imagine you'd have a variety of feelings. Probably you would feel some relief about the possibility of finally being able to put down the pack, but perhaps anger and frustration as well for all the time lost carrying around what was not yours to carry.

Laying down the outdated pack of beliefs can be disconcerting at first. We are creatures of habit, and it takes conscious intention to shift out of old patterns—even when we know they are harmful. It might take days, months, or years to master the ability to completely say good-bye to the faulty beliefs that create that pack of pain. But eventually the freedom starts to feel so good that the reasons for continuing to carry that old familiar pack of pain fade away.

The more you practice listening to your intuitive wisdom and empathic signals, mastering the tools I have outlined to fact-check and protect yourself, the stronger you will become. And the more you honestly express whatever feelings arise in the process of jettisoning those outdated beliefs and coping skills, the more accurate your intuitive voice will become. Squashing and silencing our grief does not help. Feeling all the feelings, including grief, that accompany your personal story will set you free and make access to this gift even clearer. I encourage you to feel it all honestly and with compassion for yourself. Cleaning out old wounds can be painful work, but the personal gains of coming home to your full authentic power are well worth all of the work.

When an Intuitive Child Summons the Return of Your Intuitive Self

When an adult intuitive has a relationship with a highly intuitive child, the result can be alchemical. This alchemy is not limited to the biological parenting relationship, but can also be touched off by having a relative, client, student, or friend who is a young intuitive. If your own intuitive gifts have been suppressed until this point in your life, knowing and caring about a child who innocently lives from this place of awareness can be a powerful mirror of those abilities within yourself. It provides an opportunity to get straight with this inner gift and stop suppressing or judging this trait, if that has been the case.

If an unconscious barrier exists to our own intuitive gifts, it will probably play out in some fashion in our interactions with the child. Maybe it plays out by zoning out, judging, or suppressing the messages or perceptions that the child invites. Alternatively, our heartfelt connection to the child can inspire a recommitment to living an intuitive life. Being present to the intuitive child allows for simultaneously reparenting that part of our inner self, or inner child, and meeting the child's needs.

If you have a child who struggles with the trait, some familiar pains from your own childhood might surface. Maybe a longing resurfaces of wishing that someone in your childhood had spotted your abilities and been able to speak with you about what you were experiencing. If you never received this degree of being seen for such a dynamic dimension of who you are, and you have not received this level of mirroring yet in your life, it may be time to find an adult relationship that can fill this need. Finding a therapist who is aware of this kind of healing or even a friend who knows the terrain well can be a great resource in filling this need. Filling your own intuitive cup and knowing what it feels like to be witnessed and supported is also fuel for being able to do the same for the child in your life. It is never too late to fill this cup for yourself and harness the creative power of this trait in your life.

In addition to the relationships that can help heal old wounds from childhood, you can also benefit from building an intuitive tribe. These are people who share, or at least value and can appreciate, your intuitive abilities. These are friends with whom you don't need to worry about sharing the depths of who you are. You don't need to hide. With these kindred spirits, you can share the ups and downs of living with heightened abilities and enjoy the support of others who know the lay of the land.

The Benefits of Making Peace with the Gift

If you are an adult intuitive who resonates with the ideas of this book, and especially this chapter, I want to offer you heartfelt support for reigniting your intuitive, empathic gifts. You are on the journey of awakening your own wise intuitive resource and freeing the authentic expression of who you are.

Learning how to regulate the challenges of this trait can free up a wealth of energy that yields many positive benefits. One of the benefits is having more energy available to do what you love and to connect to inner truth and guidance. You can experience clearer, more congruent communication and less fear. Being in tune to your own sensitivities, boundaries, and needs also provides information to use in being proactive about those needs—instead of always needing to recover from life. Listening to your own needs and meeting those needs on a regular basis holds the promise of feeling more alive and positive. It eliminates, or greatly shortens, the recovery time of the stressful components of this trait.

Ideally, I hold the vision of more and more adult intuitives feeling the freedom and strength to enjoy their gifts and be role models for to-day's youth. Living in harmony with this trait is very powerful, and we need not fear this power—in ourselves, or in our children. With our own intuitive empowerment comes a place of maturity with the gift that we can pass on to today's children.

in closing

Highly intuitive children come with many surprises and challenges for their parents—and great delights. Seeing life through the eyes of an intuitive, empathic child can open our own eyes to life's larger wonders, meanings, and questions. Intuitive children challenge the conventional, both in parenting and in life. They see what others do not see, they feel where others do not feel, and they perceive doorways of perception that others do not perceive. When we are open to their gifts and help them face their unique challenges with love and support, intuitive children thrive.

Sometimes you and your child might feel isolated because of the abilities and perspectives that your child possesses. Please remember that you are not alone, nor is your child. If intuitive children were that rare, there would be no use for—let alone interest in—a book such as this one. My hope is that in time we will all see a growing understanding, acceptance, and support for these children and the heightened abilities that they possess.

At this point in time on our planet, I dream that all children—including those we've focused on in this book—will retain and share their gifts in life. It is my sincere hope that the information and skills you have learned from reading this book will be of great benefit to you and also to your highly intuitive child as she develops, grows, and shares her gifts with the world.

endnotes

introduction

1. Elizabeth Lloyd Mayer, *Extraordinary Knowing: Science, Skepticism, and the Inexplicable Powers of the Human Mind* (New York: Bantam Books, 2007), 80–82.

chapter 1

1. The use of the term *trait* in this work refers to a distinguishing personality characteristic or predisposition and not as a biological trait that is passed down genetically.

chapter 2

1. Gavin DeBecker, *The Gift of Fear: Survival Skills That Protect Us from Violence* (New York: Little Brown and Company, 1997), 13.
2. Ibid., 12.
3. Ibid., 70.

chapter 3

1. Daniel Goleman, *Social Intelligence: The Revolutionary New Science of Human Relationships* (New York: Bantam, 2006), 41.
2. Ibid., 42.
3. Valerie Gazzola, Lisa Aziz-Zadeh, and Christian Keysers, "Emapthy and the Somatotopic Auditory Mirror System in Humans," *Current Biology* 16, no. 18 (September 2006): 1824–1829; Rowan Hooper, "Spectrum of Empathy Found in the Brain," NewScientist.com (September 18, 2006).

4. Stephen Hall, "Is Buddhism Good for Your Health?" *The New York Times,* (September 14, 2003).

chapter 4

1. Paul Foxman, *The Worried Child: Recognizing Anxiety in Children and Helping Them Heal* (Alameda, CA: Hunter House, 2004).
2. Susan Crockenberg and Esther Leerkes. "Infant Temperament (Reactivity to Novelty) and Maternal Behavior at 6 Months Interact to Predict Later Anxious Behavior," *Development and Psychopathology* 18 (2006): 1–18.
3. Renos K. Papadopoulos, *Carl Gustav Jung: Critical Assessments* (New York: Routledge, 1992), 157.
4. Centers for Disease Control, *MMWR Weekly* 56, no. 35 (September 7, 2007): 905–908.
5. Elaine Aron, "Parenting Sensitive Children: Growing Up Gifted Is Not Easy," *Comfort Zone Online* (February 2006).
6. Ibid.
7. Joann Deak, Professional Training in San Francisco, 2007. Joanne Deak is coauthor, with Teresa Baker, of *Girls Will Be Girls: Raising Confident and Courageous Daughters* (New York: Hyperion Books, 2002).
8. Elaine Aron, *The Highly Sensitive Child: Helping Our Children Thrive When the World Overwhelms Them* (New York: Broadway Books, 2002). Characteristics of highly sensitive children compared with intuitive children based on the parent's questionnaire titled "Is Your Child Highly Sensitive?"; Carol Stock Kranowitz, *The Out of Sync Child: Recognizing and Coping with Sensory Processing Disorder* (New York: Perigree Books, 2005), 9–11.
9. Ibid., 11.
10. Ibid., 21

chapter 5

1. Elaine Aron, *The Highly Sensitive Child: Helping Our Children Thrive When the World Overwhelms Them* (New York: Broadway Books, 2002). Characteristics of highly sensitive children compared with intuitive children based on the parent's questionnaire titled "Is Your Child Highly Sensitive?" Preface.
2. Holly Guzman, live interview conducted in Santa Cruz, California, March 2008.

chapter 7

1. Chris Mercogliano and Kim Debus, "Expressing Life's Wisdom: Nurturing Heart-Brain Development Starting with Infants," *Journal of Family Life* 5, no. 1 (1999).

chapter 8

1. Basil Johnston, *Ojibway Heritage* (Toronto: McClelland and Stewart, 1976), 69–72.
2. Malcolm Margolin, "Indian Pedagogy: A Look at Traditional California Indian Teaching Techniques," *Sacred Fire, The Modern Voice of Ancient Tradition* no. 6 (September 2007): 12–18; Malcolm Margolin, "Indian Pedagogy: A Look at Traditional California Indian Teaching Techniques," taken from *Ecological Literacy: Educating Our Children for a Sustainable World,* ed. Michael K. Stone and Zenobia Barlow (Center for Ecoliteracy and Collective Heritage Institute, 2005).

chapter 10

1. Edward Benton-Banai, *The Mishomis Book: The Voice of the Ojibway* (Hayward: WI: Indian Country Communications Inc., 1988), 78.
2. Matthew B. James, live interview conducted in Honolulu, Hawaii, February 18, 2008.
3. Liberth Angaangaq, telephone interview by author, April 2, 2008.
4. Mercedes B. Longfellow, telephone interview by author, May 7, 2008.

suggested reading

intuition and children's spirituality

Choquette, Sonia. *The Wise Child: A Spiritual Guide to Nurturing Your Child's Intuition.* New York: Three Rivers Press, 1999.

Hart, Tobin. *The Secret Spiritual World of Children: The Breakthrough Discovery that Profoundly Alters Our Conventional View of Children's Mystical Experiences.* Novato, CA: New World Library, 2003.

Mayer, Elizabeth Lloyd. *Extraordinary Knowing: Science, Skepticism, and the Inexplicable Powers of the Human Mind.* New York: Bantam Books, 2007.

Orloff, Judith. *Positive Energy: 10 Extraordinary Prescriptions for Transforming Fatigue, Stress & Fear into Vibrance, Strength & Love.* New York: Harmony Books, 2004.

Painton, Molly. *Encouraging Your Child's Spiritual Intelligence.* New York: Atria Books, 2007.

Sinetar, Marsha. *Spiritual Intelligence: What We Can Learn From the Early Awakening Child.* New York: Orbis Books, 2000.

intuitive thinkers

Palladino, Lucy Jo. *The Edison Trait: Saving the Spirit of Your Free Thinking Child in a Conforming World.* In hardcover edition with a new title release for the softcover edition: *Dreamers, Discoverers and Dynamos: How to Help the Child Who Is Bright, Bored and Having Trouble in School.* New York: Ballantine Books, 1999.

sensitivity

Aron, Elaine. *The Highly Sensitive Child: Helping Our Children Thrive When the World Overwhelms Them.* New York: Broadway Books, 2002.

————. *The Highly Sensitive Person*. New York: Broadway Books, 1997.

art and meditation resources
for use with children

Capacchione, Lucia. *The Creative Journal for Children: A Guide for Parents, Teachers and Counselors*. Boston: Shambhala Publications, 1982.

Murdock, Maureen. *Spinning Inward: Using Guided Imagery with Children for Learning, Creativity and Relaxation*. Boston: Shambhala Publications, 1987.

anxiety resources

Chansky, Tamar. *Freeing Your Child from Anxiety: Powerful, Practical Solutions to Overcome Your Child's Fears, Worries, and Phobias*. New York: Broadway Books, 2004.

Foxman, Paul. *The Worried Child: Recognizing Anxiety in Children and Helping Them Heal*. Alameda, CA: Hunter House, 2004.

parenting

Deak, JoAnn. *Girls Will Be Girls: Raising Confident and Courageous Daughters*. New York: Hyperion, 2002.

Kurcinka, Mary Sheedy. *Raising Your Spirited Child: A Guide for Parents Whose Child Is More Intense, Sensitive, Perceptive, Persistent, and Energetic*. New York: Harper Perrenial, 1998.

Miller, Alice. *The Drama of the Gifted Child: The Search for the True Self*. New York: Basic, 1994.

Pearce, Joseph. *The Biology of Transcendence*. Rochester, VT: Park Street Press, 2002.

Porro, Barbara. *Talk It Out: Conflict Resolution in the Elementary Classroom*. Alexandria, VA: Association of Supervision and Curriculum Development, 1996.

emotional and social intelligence

Goleman, Daniel. *Social Intelligence: The Revolutionary New Science of Human Relationships*. New York: Bantam, 2006.

————. *Emotional Intelligence: Why It Matters More than IQ*. New York: Bantam, 1995.

sensory processing disorder

Heller, Sharon. *Too Loud, Too Bright, Too Fast, Too Tight: What to Do If You Are Sensory Defensive in an Overstimulating World.* New York: Harper Collins, 2002.

Horowitz, Lynn, and Cecile Röst. *Helping Hyperactive Kids: A Sensory Integration Approach.* Alameda, CA: Hunter House, 2007.

Kranowitz, Carol Stock. *The Out of Sync Child: Recognizing and Coping with Sensory Integration Dysfunction.* New York: Perigree Publishing, 1998.

type and temperament

Armstrong, Thomas. *In Their Own Way: Discovering and Encouraging Your Child's Personal Learning Style.* Los Angeles: Jeremy Tarcher, 1987.

Murphy, Elizabeth. *The Developing Child: Using Jungian Type to Understand Children.* Mountain View, CA: Davies-Black Publishing, 1992.

Tieger, Paul, and Barron-Tieger, Barbara. *Nurture by Nature: Understand Your Child's Personality Type—And Become a Better Parent.* Boston: Little Brown & Co., 1997.

suicide prevention

National Suicide Prevention Lifeline Toll Free Number: (800) 273-TALK (273-8255) or (800) Suicide (999-9999) and Suicide.org.

To learn more about workshops and services provided by Catherine Crawford, please visit www.lifepassage.com.

index

CPSIA information can be obtained at www.ICGtesting.com
Printed in the USA
BVOW07s1338170615

405048BV00026B/381/P